Eternal Makeovers

KAITEE LUSK

© 2006 by Kaitee Lusk. All rights reserved.

Pleasant Word (a division of WinePress Publishing, PO Box 428, Enumclaw, WA 98022) functions only as book publisher. As such, the ultimate design, content, editorial accuracy, and views expressed or implied in this work are those of the author.

No part of this publication may be reproduced, stored in a retrieval system or transmitted in any way by any means—electronic, mechanical, photocopy, recording or otherwise—without the prior permission of the copyright holder, except as provided by USA copyright law.

Unless otherwise noted, all Scriptures are taken from the Holy Bible, New International Version, Copyright © 1973, 1978, 1984 by the International Bible Society. Used by permission of Zondervan Publishing House. The "NIV" and "New International Version" trademarks are registered in the United States Patent and Trademark Office by International Bible Society.

Scripture references marked KJV are taken from the King James Version of the Bible.

Scripture references marked NASB are taken from the New American Standard Bible, © 1960, 1963, 1968, 1971, 1972, 1973, 1975, 1977 by The Lockman Foundation. Used by permission.

ISBN 1-4141-0573-8
Library of Congress Catalog Card Number: 2005907965

Table of Contents

Foreword and Acknowledgements.................... vii
Introduction xiii

Chapter 1: The Extra 747 Pilot
   Explosive Decompressions........................... 15
Chapter 2: Big Time for Andrew,
   Gary, and Peter..25
Chapter 3: God, Where Are You? 35
Chapter 4: How Did You Get That Scar? 41
Chapter 5: Ironic Detour 47
Chapter 6: Sudden Eclipse 57
Chapter 7: President Ferdinand E. Marcos........67
Chapter 8: In My Heart Too! 91
Chapter 9: Heaven versus Richard Crabbe......... 99
Chapter 10: If You Don't Know, You Aren't..... 107
Chapter 11: The Eleventh Hour!....................... 111

Chapter 12: Ride'm Cowboy 127
Chapter 13: From Chicken Bones
  to Ironman...................................... 137
Chapter 14: Big Jim Oren and the
  Little Green Submarine 155
Chapter 15: The Anchor Man.......................... 165
Chapter 16: Fire and Ice.................................... 171
Chapter 17: Special Child 183
Chapter 18: Status Symbol to
  Status Symbol.. 195
Chapter 19: Jodi's Rocky Soil......................... 203
Chapter 20: I Just Want Them to
  Know Him! 215
Chapter 21: Giant Hands 219

Foreword and Acknowledgements

How can I list the innumerable friends, relatives, and acquaintances that were a part of this incredible journey the Lord set me on? The truth is, I cannot. Yet, I would be totally remiss if I did not mention those directly associated with my literary career, without whom this first book would not have been possible.

Before I'd ever heard of Mt. Hermon and its annual Christian Writers Conference, I received an invitation to attend one in April or May of 1985, the funds miraculously coming from a totally unexpected source. Within one week, both Jerry Jenkins of Moody Press and Lori Sorenson of Decision Magazine said, "You need to write for the Lord." Two months later, at a singles conference in Anaheim, California Luci Swindoll reaffirmed their statements with, "If you don't take that talent out of the ground where you've buried it, I wouldn't want to be in your shoes."

Within a year that statement propelled me into Christian Courier Ministries, Inc. (a corporation formed by the insistence and assistance of a brother-in-Christ, Attorney Vance VanTassell.) My first article, "God, Where Are You?" and those that followed are evidence of His amazing love and miraculous miracles.

And it was that amazing love (as there were no funds) that poured over me by the ministry staff, Kent and Diane Sanctuary, Dave and Nancy Doty, and Jimmy White. Their countless and sometimes all night vigils to make deadlines gave me the courage to continue. I can also vividly recall the awe I felt as Senator Tim Leslie and Assemblyman Larry Bowler promoted *The Christian Courier, The Encourager* during their campaign trails throughout the Sacramento area. (Whoever heard of a politician promoting a Christian magazine during their campaigns? P.S. They both won!)

Could any of the above been accomplished without prayer? You have to pray and believe to receive, and you can't receive unless you act upon what you believe. I had the most incredible prayer partners. I want to thank my family, especially my children, Mary, Nancy, and Heather and their husbands, Ralph, Richard, and Marc who stood by me through many a storm and discouragement, together with some very dear friends from Sacramento, Tom and Vivian

Foreword and Acknowledgements

Sarmento (who were also responsible for sending me on several of the missionary journeys referred to in these stories), Steve and Elva Burlingham, Tony and Rosemarie Pavelka, Trisha Wood, Maria Viviano, Tom and Lisa Hill, and Tom and Janis Mills.

In addition, I had prayer warriors – they are known as intercessors – who fight and fast against all odds, no matter what time of day or night, and who believe by faith that with God all things are possible, no matter what the circumstances. These acknowledgements are dedicated to the following: my chief warrior, Vincent Fry, who to this very day stands in the gap for me and this ministry on a daily basis, together with my VP and Editor in Chief, Allison Jones, and VP, Konny Garrett. The list is not short, but I with joy also mention Dave and Debbie Cronin, Gini and Barry Dower, the Daniels, Copelands, Larsons, Brenes, Gloria Lopez, and Rhea Padellford, my Truckee prayer trackers.

His ways are not our ways and I am, as usual, in awe of the Potter's plans to accomplish His purposes. He knew Maui was the place He wanted this journey to climax into the very first book of books to be published in witness of His eternal and unfathomable makeovers; makeovers in the lives of those who believed and received the amazing love He shed for them.

To that end, this first book is also in memory of a very dear friend, Jeri Jaques. The Lord took Jeri home (at her request) on my birthday last year, November 14, 2004. It was Jeri's amazing love for the Lord that caused her to pursue me (and others) to "stop lingering at the gate" and finish the race He set before us. She pushed all of us nonstop. She gave me no rest until I took a loan, paid off my car, bought a computer, and set about getting the Lord's work done.

When Jeri went home my book was not done, but my heavenly Father was well aware of that. He quickly brought Carol Dawson to the rescue. (Carol spent countless hours praying and nurturing me back to health following a serious medical emergency and surgery). Right along with Carol came Dean and Jan Erickson who provided my "Upper Room" Ohana where I could quietly write and worship the Lord. When computer snags and hang-ups tormented me, Kim Paulsen and Pastors Craig Englert and Kit Lauer came to the rescue. Janna Schlag, musician and photographer followed. (I lost track of the countless hours she has given in editing.) And, to my astonishment, then came Lisa Kim Bryant, my answer to prayer, my special angel, and computer geek as she calls herself. If it weren't for her and the staff at WinePress Publishing, in particular, Abigail Davidson, my project manager and Janice Robeson, production assistant, this computer rookie would never have been able to get this book into print. Their priceless sacrifices of time and input have been invaluable.

When Kevin and Nancy Boorman, Jacqueline Kelly, Joyce Spencer, and Kris Kozub appeared on the scene, I was truly in awe of the grace I was

Foreword and Acknowledgements

being given. Not one of them knew each other. Yet each came and said, "The Lord said to assist you in this work." And assist they did. In ways I never expected.

Rick Defer and Jodi Kuhnmuench (their stories are part of this book) came next, and then my brother, Eric Leiser, who I recall saying quite a way back, "Kaitee, I never knew you could write; keep up the good work." It was this "good work" that caused my wonderful brother to believe. I never realized the impact all the stories I'd sent him in the past had made.

I cannot, in all conscience, close this foreword and its acknowledgements without thanking the Lord for all those who so freely and willingly gave permission for their stories to be shared so others can experience and realize what an eternal makeover can truly mean if they can but believe and receive.

Kaitee M. Lusk

Introduction

The journeys you are about to take as you enter the very hearts of those who have so graciously permitted me to share their stories are phenomenal. You may find yourself living and experiencing some of their emotional, mental, financial, and even physical struggles. In some instances, you may even say to yourself, *That's me. That's what happened to me.*

Their stories are alive because they are experienced over and over again in the lives of people all over the world. Motion pictures are designed to draw their audiences into the very lives of the actors and actresses and the roles they are portraying, and the journeys in this book even more so because they are not fictitious. They actually happened and are continuing to happen.

Each story is different, yet similar. You may laugh with some, cry with others. You might identify with those who have lost a child, suffered broken bones, broken homes or hearts, or suffered seemingly unending pain.

They are the stories of the journey of life and each individual's struggle to find the answer to what lies beyond what they know will eventually come to an end. They are journeys that bring the priceless hope of an eternal home to the reality of their hearts.

The stories in this book are true. The people are real. Their lives have been extremely changed and made over spiritually, mentally, emotionally, and sometimes even physically. They attribute their phenomenal transformation to the miraculous power of God through the Holy Spirit. Therefore, this book is dedicated to the Great Spirit of all heaven and earth, God the Father, and His only Son, Jesus Christ, without whom none of these stories would be possible.

CHAPTER ONE

THE EXTRA 747 PILOT EXPLOSIVE DECOMPRESSIONS

Dave Cronin, Captain of Flight 811

David Cronin, a United Airlines 747 captain, experienced two explosive decompressions. One left a huge cavity in the cockpit of his heart; the other, a gaping hole in the fuselage of his 747. One changed his life; the other made him a national hero. Both left an eternal impact!

I drove fast, flew fast, and lived fast. My goal was to be captain of my ship, master of my fate, and I was flying high until September 1988 when my second marriage blew up without warning. That explosive decompression tore the door off my reason for living. For the first time, my ship was sinking and my fate hung in the balance. It took the wind out of my sails, life from my spirit, and left me in a stunned and speechless vacuum in the shattering wake of its destruction. No earthly medication could dull the pain of the humiliation that slashed at my pride and reduced my self-esteem to mincemeat. Anger, hatred, and bitterness took control, and self-pity was close by. Where did I go wrong? I'd filled my heart with selfish treasures, leaving no room for God or anyone else. I had deceived myself into believing I had it made, and I began to search for answers. Jeremiah17:9 says, "The heart is deceitful above all things and beyond cure…"

Dad, who always took us to church, died when I was sixteen, and though we continued to go after his death, God was always very distant to me. With my sister in college, Mom and I were left to care for the chickens, goats, ducks, geese, and three acres of land at our Trumbull, Connecticut home. This

The Extra 747 Pilot Explosive Decompressions

didn't leave much time for what I wanted to do. I'd always loved racing, adventure, and things that moved fast. So, just before my last year of college, I applied to the United States Air Force for pilot training. That dream came true in November 1951 when they gave me my class date – Class 53A. At graduation in 1953, I received my Silver Wings and Commission as 2nd Lieutenant. I couldn't wait to fly; my heart was heaven bound (but not for the Lord). I still visited God on Sundays, but during the week imitated most twenty-three year old single guys with lots of partying, girls, etc.

In December 1954, another dream came true when I was accepted as a pilot for United Airlines. My training was to begin December 10 and I was on top of the world, but just before that, I had another surprise! I was going to become a father. My dream seemed to disintegrate in mid-air. I'd been dating pretty heavily, but marriage and a family were not part of my physical and emotional "fuselage" at this time. My mental instruments went crazy over this threatening detour in my future, but I got married with the determination to make it in spite of the circumstances.

Donna was only twenty and I was twenty-five. She was very naïve, and I was very macho and never once did I consider my share of the blame. I vented my anger on Donna and made life really tough for her. We spent Christmas in an $85 a month motel room where she was so sentimental, she kept the Christmas tree up until there were no needles left on it. We got rid of it around March and, three months later, on July 19, 1955, our first daughter, Kimberly, was born. When she was just about ten months old, Donna gave birth to our second girl, Kathy. In 1959 Kelly came along, and in 1961 Karen joined the family. Right after Karen's birth, I went to Europe for a year as a fighter pilot, came back in 1962 to fly with United and three years later our fifth daughter, Kris, was born.

On the surface, I was a model father who took the kids to church, provided a nice home, nice clothes, etc. but my tainted image was overlooked. In reality, I was an overly strict (and mostly absent) father who ran his family like a military organization. You just don't (or shouldn't) treat little girls that way. Whenever I'd come home from a trip with United, I'd jump into my National Guard outfit, drive one hundred miles to Massachusetts and fly for them. Then, I'd drive back home and get back into my United uniform to fly for them; it never ended. They had everything except me and my love. In fact, the love was replaced by fear. They were scared to see me come home from a trip because I'd go berserk if they left the lights on in the cellar and other trivial things like that. I was the macho fighter pilot and the macho father and disciplinarian. "Do as I say," was my motto. I was the wage earner and I was in charge! I made sure they got everything I wanted them to have but not what they needed, a husband and father. "Things" took the place where I should have been.

The Extra 747 Pilot Explosive Decompressions

When UA promoted me to captain, I moved us into a new fifty-four hundred square foot house on the Trumbull waterfront (a very elite area). I think we were the beginning of the yuppie generation. Was I ever proud! The girls had their own sailboats, etc. and it was a great place to raise kids but I didn't know the meaning of the word; I'd left that job mostly to Donna. With all we had, things got worse and Donna began seeing a psychiatrist, but he couldn't give her what she needed from me. My selfish attitude built lots of resentment in Donna and the girls so that by the time they were teenagers, Donna couldn't handle it anymore. Finally, when I asked her if she still loved me and she didn't answer, I moved out and divorced her.

Within my new little condo I was quick to rationalize my behavior, convincing myself I had done the right thing. My out-of-sight, out-of-mind theory worked great and this deception took flight on a pleasure trip that lasted seven years. From 1974 to 1981 I thought I was the swingingest bachelor on earth with lots of time off, lots of women, parties, and money. I kept flying high with lots of skiing, sailing, bicycling, hiking, traveling, and scuba diving all over the world; I denied myself nothing. "What good will it be for a man if he gains the whole world, yet forfeits his soul?" (Matt. 16:26).

In 1981 I met my second wife and moved to Nevada, where we were entranced by the New Age movement and its fortune tellers, etc. (just like Babylon many years ago; same package but with a different ribbon.) I even paid five hundred dollars to have her channeled to a spirit guide. In 1986 I began flying a route from Los Angeles, California to Auckland, New Zealand and Sydney, Australia. During the spring of that year, my co-pilot gave me a card that read, "If you want to be saved, you have to accept Jesus Christ as your Lord…" I put the card in my wallet and forgot about it until the night my marriage ended leaving that sudden huge cavity with no answers. That's when the heartaches I'd sown in my first marriage began to jet across the mirror of my mind. The Bible says, "A man reaps what he sows" (Gal. 6:7), and reap I did! But, unlike me who did not show compassion and ran away, God opened a door and I came across that card in my wallet. I read it over and over and over again, saying those words. I decided that if God could take control of my life, this was the time to do it. I prayed the prayer on the card asking Jesus to come into my life and forgive my sins. Then I took a long walk and meditated on what I had done.

Two days later, I woke up with a tremendous desire to go to church. It wouldn't go away, and on Sunday I found myself up at 7:00 A.M. heading for Truckee where I somehow found Calvary Chapel, a church I'd heard about from a friend. When I got there, they were praising and singing and at first I thought, *Wow! My New Age spirit guides led me here.* When Pastor Larson began talking about marriage and faithfulness, I began weeping in the back of the church. And, when I heard him say, "If the Lord

The Extra 747 Pilot Explosive Decompressions

accepts you, He will remove the evil elements from your life," my heart melted. I realized then that it was the Holy Spirit moving in my life and not some New Age spirit guide that had led me to this church. God had wanted me here after I received Christ as my Savior so I could learn more about Him. Two months later, in November 1988, I was baptized in a hot tub in the middle of a snowstorm on Dr. John Hejny's back deck in Truckee. A few days later I purchased my first Bible and spent hours every day reading it. I even took it back and forth on my daily flights; I was so eager to learn everything in it.

Six months later on February 24, 1989, I encountered my second unexpected explosive decompression as my 747, Flight 811 traveled from Honolulu to Auckland, New Zealand. This is where my new faith in God was tested and the Lord revealed His awesome power proving that though I might be captain of my ship, I was definitely not master of my fate. John 15:5 says, "Apart from Me, you can do nothing," and in Matthew 19:26, "With God all things are possible." As we took off on that incredible journey with 230,000 pounds of fuel, 336 passengers and 15 flight attendants, we found ourselves in the middle of a severe thunderstorm with lots of lightening. At 10,000 feet I normally turn off the seat belt sign so passengers can move around, but something inside said, *Remember the storm—leave it on!* I was glad I did because between 22,000 and 23,000 feet I felt a bump followed by a tremendous explosion and decompression that left a huge ten by twenty-one foot hole in the fuselage. Nine passengers and some luggage were instantly blown out. One stewardess miraculously escaped the same fate; she had been thrown to the floor by the explosion as she was coming down the aisle and was being helplessly drawn to the opening when she latched onto the steel bottom of one of the passenger seats just a few feet from the gaping hole and held fast until the plane landed.

In addition to the missing passengers and luggage, the blast sucked out all our oxygen bottles and left number three engine inoperative but, incredibly, the plane held together. I said a quick prayer and then concentrated on what to do. My next thought was to drop the landing gear and get into some breathable air, but again, a still small voice within said, *Wait!* which later turned out to be a wise decision because number four engine went on fire and had to be shut down. This left us with only two engines as we descended 1500 feet a minute with no way of being able to arrest the rate of descent. It was like being in a 400 mile an hour tornado. I didn't think about it at the time, but knew later that we had an extra pilot on board. God had been with us. He'd been in the cockpit guiding me and was the one who enabled us to remain calm and who directed the incredible teamwork.

The flight attendants were fantastic. Taking no regard for their own lives, they made sure all passengers had life preservers on, as we didn't know if we were coming down on water or land. When we finally did land twenty-two minutes later, we were able to evacuate everyone in less than forty-five seconds with no broken bones. Yes, God had been in charge and we made it because our extra pilot, Jesus Christ, was right there with us saying, "Never will I leave you. Never will I forsake you" (Heb. 13:5). His goals are now my goals and I've given Him complete charge of my life. I'm no longer Dave Cronin, captain of my ship, master of my fate but Dave Cronin, Christ's co-pilot. "Those who hope in the Lord will renew their strength; they will soar on wings like eagles. They will run and not grow weary; they will walk and not be faint" (Is. 40:31).

In the Bible, the Lord often revealed His plans before they came into being. After the accident, the following vision was revealed and confirmed: A Christian woman who started a prayer group about one and a half years prior to the explosion (and who prayed daily for the planes that flew over her house), woke up at 6:46 A.M. on February 11 after experiencing a terrible nightmare. (It was thirteen days prior to the accident. The nightmare was so intense it took her one and a half hours to compose herself before she could call her friend on the telephone. The vision was incredibly vivid—shortly after take-off a charter jet was in desperate trouble and in need of emergency assistance. She saw fire on the right side of the aircraft; the pilot was having a very difficult time getting the airplane back to the field. She next saw herself on the roof of a high building; a man was standing to her right with his left hand on her right shoulder. He was telling her that the pilot will get the airplane back and he will be OK. Could this "man" have been the extra pilot?

Coincidence? The woman's name happens to be Theresa Cronin Cook. She is no relation to our pilot, Captain Cronin, but was definitely heard and answered by God because of her prayers.

How about you? Is the Lord in control of your life, or are you flying on a course bound for destruction and an explosive decompression that will blow you out of eternity? Will you let Christ into the cockpit of your heart and give Him the controls? He'll help you fly a new course to eternal destinations if you'll let Him be the pilot in charge of your life. Jesus said, "I stand at the door and knock, if anyone hears my voice and opens the door, I will come in" (Rev. 3:20). If you want to become a Christian and fly with Jesus, with all your heart, and by faith, pray the following prayer: Dear Jesus, I open the door of my life. Please come in, forgive my sins, and take control of my life. I receive you as my Savior and Lord and ask you to fill me with your Holy Spirit and accept me as your child.

CHAPTER TWO

BIG TIME FOR ANDREW, GARY, AND PETER

This was 'Big Time' but my big moment was the beginning of my downfall, because I really lost it, badly!"

Andrew Langsford was only nineteen when a real popular artist, one of New Zealand's biggies, asked him to play with his band. This was the opportunity of a lifetime, a claim to fame that he readily accepted. But why did he fall, and where do Gary and Peter fit into this picture? Andrew's story is typical of youngsters seeking that breakthrough to fame, to be somebody. He shares it in the hope of sparing others the misery he experienced.

Mom and Dad were wonderful and very supportive of me and my brothers, Gary and Peter. When I was thirteen, even though I did well in school and had a happy home life, I wanted to be accepted by the other kids. One night at a neighbor's home, one of the older boys asked if I wanted to try some marijuana and I said yes. It didn't seem like any big deal to me but that's where it all started.

Using this drug seemed normal because everyone did it and, since we weren't Christians, I didn't think my parents would mind. But then, I didn't tell them about it either. The marijuana quickly took away my desire to study and I exerted just barely enough effort to get passing grades. I continued to cruise through school until I was sixteen. Then I left and began touring with my brother's band where I got involved in music, but this also enhanced my drug use and started me into stronger stuff. The guys in the band were all older and although my brother

Big Time for Andrew, Gary, and Peter

Gary watched out for me, he couldn't watch out for me all the time. Consequently, I got into a lot more drugs. I kept trying all kinds of things that seemed like more fun. I kept thinking, *You've got to do this man, people will like you more if you do; it's going to make you feel better and you're going to have a good time.* Pretty soon I didn't care about anyone. Even though I always loved my family, I really cared more about myself now and it didn't matter if what I was doing was hurting them. All I wanted was to satisfy my own cravings.

During the first three years of this adventure in music and drugs, I was fine and healthy. I didn't have any problems and still had a good family life, and at age nineteen, even got a big break in my music career. A real popular artist, one of the biggies in New Zealand, wanted me to play guitar with his band. This was big time, my big moment, and I jumped at the chance to join this popular group. But the beginning of my claim to fame was the beginning of my downfall because here I lost it – badly – and went down hill. I began touring with this band and eventually got into really hard drugs. I'd graduated to the major leagues, which basically made me a complete wreck. The devil was having a field day because I was sick all the time. I couldn't eat and I withdrew into my own little world. This is what drugs do to you. You can't remember things. Drugs are all you think about, all you care about, and all you want. You're in total bondage to them.

About this time, Mom became a Christian and began praying for me. She began witnessing to me all the time and didn't hold back as you would expect. I remember her giving me lots of tapes and posters. I never once thought she had flipped out or gone overboard being religious, and I never brushed her off but listened with great interest. Though I didn't accept Christ, inside I kept thinking, *This is right, and I'm going to go for this one day, but not right now.* This was a difficult time for my parents, especially Mom; she knew she couldn't push me too hard. She used to hear me come home from the gigs at night and I'd be in the bathroom being sick. I was stoned, smashed, etc. but, instead of yelling at me, Mom would get up and just pray for me, and so I knew it must have been a really hard time for her. Sometimes I wasn't on drugs but only because I couldn't get them in our country. Otherwise, I would have been in worse trouble. As it was, I walked away from a couple of bad car wrecks and situations with the police; I stayed out of jail because they couldn't find any drugs on me.

God unquestionably had His hand on my life during this time and still does. Things began turning around when I met Brent, a Christian musician who, through various circumstances, came to stay at our house. He knew I was a total wreck and I knew he was a born-again Christian, but this seemed to bother neither of us, and we hit it off as friends immediately because of our common interest in music. Brent never pushed a point with me but always brought God into the conversation somehow, and this is when I started getting hungry for God. I was twenty-one years old and really sick of what I was doing. I was empty spiritually and physically, emotionally and mentally tired. God chose this time to knock at my door; He knew I'd be ready to answer. One night an evangelist by the name of Barry Smith came to town. He was talking about the end times, which really intrigued me. When Brent invited me to come hear him speak, I accepted the invitation because I was curious and also because I thought, *He's a nice guy and comes to see me play and do my thing, the least I can do is to see what's happening on his turf.* As I walked out the door, a strange thought crossed my mind. I couldn't explain it and I didn't know what to expect but somehow felt, *I'm going to be different when I come back.*

At the meeting, I was a little uncomfortable because I'd never been to a church before except a wedding and funeral. But, in spite of feeling strange, I was all ears when Barry began to speak and listened with intent to his message (like a dry sponge soaking up water). At the end, everyone was standing up singing beautiful worship songs and God's Spirit drew me as the pastor began to say, "Is there anyone here that would like to accept Christ?"

I wanted God so badly that before the sentence was finished, I was out of my seat and running down to accept Christ before about two thousand people. I said, "God, here I am. I'm yours now Lord. Here I am; forgive me. I am a sinner. I open my heart to you now. I want to be one of your children. Work in my life. I'm yours from this point on." I felt a great relief.

This is what I'd been waiting for my whole life. I was happy and had a ton of questions. Like a new baby, I was hungry; hungry to know more about God. I couldn't wait to tell Mom. She was at the door when we walked in. I think she sensed that her prayers would be answered that night. I just gave her a hug and said something like, "Mom, I did it" and she knew I'd accepted Christ. This was a very happy time for us with lots of laughter and tears. Because of my past, the changes in me were very noticeable. "If anyone is in Christ, he is a new creation, the old has gone, the new has come" (2 Cor. 5:17).

First of all, I was off drugs straight away with no yearnings to get back on them. I left the popular big time band I was with and really began seeking what God wanted to do with my life. I also completely cut myself off from my old friends because I believed I would just be tempted to go back into old things again. (Anyone that's been into drugs shouldn't see old friends.) This is really hard to do but important because you need to get some good foundations and your feet on the ground with God. After that, God will show you if and when you are strong enough to go back and be a witness to them. We started going to a good church, and my old life continued to pass away. I made Christian friends and began hanging out with them. Later on, I started seeing some of my old buddies again. It surprised me when I told them what happened to me that they didn't think I was completely nuts. They said, "Well, that's good; that's cool." I was impressed that they still accepted me, and since they did, that perhaps they might let me witness to them.

Seven or eight years ago Christian bands were basically nonexistent in New Zealand. Aside from church worship, you couldn't find any. There was a time when I didn't play in a band at all because there were no Christian musicians and no Christian rock bands. I was very disappointed and discouraged and, in desperation, went to America in search of a Christian band to play with. I found one and because I wanted to do great things for God, thought this was the band He wanted me to be with, but it wasn't. I discovered it wasn't the type of Christian music the Lord led me over there for, but it was a time of healing and spiritual growth for me. I was there eleven months the first year and six months the following, but Immigration made it more and more difficult for me to stay and so I had to leave.

When I came home in 1989, I didn't do as well. There was no Christian stuff to do here and I got very discouraged and distressed. I got into another secular band but not back into drugs or anything like that, but I was out of fellowship with God. (If you're not going to church or reading your Bible, that's backsliding as far as I'm concerned.) That's what happened to me and for a few months; I became very spiritually dry. Yet, all this time, God stayed with me. "Never will I leave you; never will I forsake you" (Heb. 13:5). That's the great thing about God; you can take ten thousand steps away from Him, but need only one to get back and that's awesome. God's always saying, "Come on. You've blown it, but here I am."

That's when I discovered South City Church. A lot of them had come out of drugs, gangs, etc., just like me, and now they were on fire for the Lord. The young people made God and worship an especially enjoyable thing for me. They were always happy and this was nothing routine for them. The pastor, John Morgan, was about my age and became a good friend and buddy that I could count on.

Within a couple of weeks of coming back to the Lord, exciting things began happening. My oldest brother Gary wanted to come to church. He didn't say why; probably because of the change in my life and I guess he was searching. I was surprised and pleased that he wanted to come with me, and after the pastor's message, Gary melted. He became a big softie and turned to me and said, "I'd like to go up."

I said, "I'll go with you." And we stood there; arm in arm and in tears. Gary and I were always close and it gave me a great lift in my faith to see my brother come to Christ. It was a great experience.

A couple of weeks later, another amazing thing happened. My other brother, Peter, started asking questions and it wasn't long before he came to church as well. God was really watching over Peter because the first person he saw when he walked into South City Church was someone he knew, an old friend and tennis coach named Chris Russ. Seeing him put Peter right at ease and once again, when the pastor preached a salvation message, the same thing happened. Peter said, "I want to go up, will you go with me?"

I said yes and with arm and arm around each other and big tears, we celebrated Peter's acceptance of Christ – all this in about a month. This was the real "big time." What a great revival time for our whole family!

I know God is going to lead me into ministry as far as my music goes. I felt in the past that I tried to push it, so I'm totally just waiting on God's timing and spending time in prayer about it. I'm with another band right now and I believe God got me this job (which I thank Him for) because it's not easy to find work. I also thank Him for the band members who don't use drugs; I believe they, too, will come to Christ one day. They see me being a Christian and also as Andrew – as being me – and that's so important. They see that God loves me exactly as I am, and I love them. God is interested in the heart! I want to serve the Lord in music and also everyday in just letting Him use me to reach someone for Him wherever I am, wherever I go. "Come, follow me...and I will make you fishers of men" (Matt. 4:19). I don't need a guitar to tell someone about Christ, but I want to use the music He gave me for His glory. He brought the message of His love and forgiveness to me through Mom, my friend Brent, and Barry Smith. Now it's my turn.

Andrew gave up the opportunity of a lifetime to accept a lifetime opportunity that nothing in this world can match – the gift of eternal life.

Where are you in your walk with the Lord? Do you know Christ as your Savior? Has someone been trying to tell you about Him? Are you paying attention or are you too busy trying to make it "big time" on your own turf. If you want Christ as your Savior and to see your life change, you can pray the prayer Andrew did or you can use the following one: Dear Jesus, I open the door of my heart to you. Please come in, forgive my sins, and take control of my life. I receive you as my Savior and Lord and ask you to fill me with your Holy Spirit and accept me as your child.

CHAPTER THREE

GOD, WHERE ARE YOU?

As a child, Kaitee Lusk was always in church. For her that was where God lived, in a home surrounded by statutes of His angels and saints. They were there to remind her that only holy things could get close to God. She wanted to be close to Him, yet she knew she could never measure up to a saint or an angel, no matter how hard she tried.

I studied about God everyday but I never knew Him, so the building He lived in became my temporary security. I remember running there several times a week looking for answers and a lasting peace of mind I never seemed to have.

As I grew older, I didn't go as often because of guilt. I learned to smoke and drink together with acquiring some very vulgar language soon after I married. I figured God didn't want to see me anyway, and I was tired of going to confession every week only to have to go back and embarrass myself by confessing the same sins over and over again. Still, I thought I was pretty good until my first child died 24 hours after I gave birth to him. Then I thought, *I must be awful to deserve such punishment.*

Four years later, my husband left with another woman. Divorce followed, and the church said we were excommunicated—that meant condemned forever because I believed that no other church had the key to heaven. A year or so later we remarried and four years later he left again—another divorce. Totally despondent, I took my two children and moved to another state. I was alone, empty, and afraid. I tried to commit suicide twice. I didn't want to live but then again, I didn't want to die. I just wanted to escape from the unending pain of what I was living with. There was no peace, no acceptance, no future, and no more building where God lived for me to escape to.

Finally, in desperation and loneliness, I married again, only to find that I'd gone from bad to worse. My wonderful new husband had a problem – alcoholism. Life was a total torment with mental, emotional, and physical abuse for me and my two girls who were now almost eight and eleven.

By our first anniversary, I gave birth to another daughter via caesarean section. Two weeks later we moved from New Jersey to Kincheloe Air Force Base, Michigan. Upon arrival I began hemorrhaging and almost died, but miraculously, once again God spared my life. He knew what He had planned for me, but I didn't know Him. This left me crying out to God, not wanting to live the rest of my life without Him. Things got so bad one night that while I was home alone, I sat on the living room floor and cried out to God in tears. I confessed every sin I could think of, knowing I'd never remember them all and asking for forgiveness, and I remember saying to God, "God please help me. I want You and I want my family to know You, and, if I can't have You, then I don't want to live. I wish I could put You inside of me where no one could ever again say 'You can't have God, and you can't go to church because you're excommunicated.'" I continued to pray and repeat those words and then added, "If You don't take my life, I will take it and I won't fail this time because I can't live this way." I didn't understand it but within moments of that prayer, a peace came over me, and I fell sound asleep on the floor.

When I woke up I felt differently. The problems were still there but they didn't seem to matter anymore. I couldn't understand and kept thinking, *What's happened to me?* I began wondering and asking God to show me why I feel so different. (It was months later that I heard the scripture, "I stand at the door and knock. If anyone hears my voice and opens the door, I will come in" (Rev. 3:20). Unknowingly, in my depression I had basically prayed a prayer of repentance and had asked God to come in and take over my life.

Everything began to change after I did this. The next morning (Saturday) a military chaplain came to my door saying, "The women on base told me you have a real desire to go to church and I came to find out why you don't come." He happened to be (unknown to me) a born-again Catholic priest. I shared with him the details of my life and what happened the night before and how I fell asleep on the floor and woke up feeling differently. Then he smiled and nodded and said, "I have one question to ask you. If you came to church tomorrow and Jesus was handing out communion, do you think He would refuse you?"

I said, "No, I don't believe He would."

Then he said, "Well, neither will I, please come and join us."

Well, I almost fainted. I couldn't believe I was being accepted and invited to come to church. The next morning as I was getting ready, my girls looked at me and said, "Mom, where are you going?"

"To church with you," I said. They looked at me in disbelief.

"Really? How come?"

"The chaplain was here last night and he said I could come."

When it was time for communion and I started down the aisle, something very strange happened. As I stepped out from the pew and began to walk and looked at the chaplain, he disappeared and in his place I saw Jesus (or at least that's who I thought I saw). I blinked again and again, and the vision remained. And, when I got up to Him, and He handed me the bread and wine (grape juice), I took it and on the way back to my seat, I remember beginning to cry and cry and cry until my whole body was shaking. I trembled so much, and the sobbing had gotten so loud that the ushers came and took me into a back room thinking I was ill.

"What's wrong?" they asked, "Are you sick?"

"No!" I almost shouted amidst my shaking and crying. "I'm so happy, I just realized that Jesus loves me, died for me, and wants me to be part of His life, and that He will always love me." And on and on I went.

Things continued to change day by day. Every time I used a vulgar word it made me sick, every time I took a drink I developed stomach cramps; I had already given up smoking a year earlier. I felt differently toward my family and friends (even toward my husband) and experienced a new attitude toward others, which has grown through the years. I had an inner awareness of God that was ever present which was something I'd never known before. I had a desire to share this love with others and looked for the good things in people instead of the bad. When problems came, I was able to face them better, knowing God was with me. I slept peacefully at night. My life is exciting. My family saw the changes in me and I was able to share this experience with them. I'm no longer afraid of death (wondering where I'm going when I die) and neither are they. It's wonderful to see their peace and confidence knowing He is in us and with us every day, everywhere we go. I no longer have to search for God in a building and I no longer try to measure up to an angel. And, no matter what happens or where I go, I shall never, never forget this awesome, powerful, gracious heavenly Father who took a very lost, lonely despairing young mother and wrapped her in His garment of love; a Father who truly hears the cry of someone who is looking for Him with all their heart.

Although I don't deserve it, I have the assurance of knowing that though I'm not perfect and make mistakes, I belong to God, and if I were to die today, I would have a place in heaven because of His gift of eternal life. "My sheep listen to my voice. I know them and they follow me. I give them eternal life and they shall never perish" (John 10:27, 28).

If you're asking God where are you? Just remember, he's as close as the words in your mouth. Just invite Him in and He will come in.

Chapter Four

How Did You Get That Scar?

Carl, Carl where are you? Please help me.

Mary (Lusk) Loeffler might have been blind today, even dead. Instead, she's very much alive, both physically and spiritually, because the Lord knew this very tragic accident would cause her to come to Him. The story behind the scar is the story of God's love for her.

Though only thirteen years of age, Mary was babysitting for three small children on the evening of April 27, 1972. She was alone earlier in the evening, but around seven thirty in the evening a friend from her algebra class stopped by to get help with his homework. Just before she and Carl began studying, she went upstairs to put the children to bed.

"It was cool for April, and I decided to close an open window in their room. I didn't notice a crack that split the pane right across the middle, from top to bottom. When I pulled, the window slid easily for a few inches, then stuck. I pulled again, only harder this time. Nothing happened. By the third try, I had become a bit impatient. I got a firm hold of the handgrip and pulled with all my strength. Then I heard the gritty, scratching noise of broken glass rubbing together. I looked up to see where it was coming from. The huge pane was already on its way to the floor. It came toward me horizontally, and I closed my eyes and turned my head."

As she turned her head, the edge of the glass sliced Mary right between the eyes and down the bridge of her nose. Somehow, the glass incredibly turned from horizontal to vertical during its descent. If the glass had struck at almost any other angle, she might have been permanently blind in one or both eyes. Because there was no pain, she didn't realize what had happened, but when she reached up to rub her forehead, she felt something wet. Her fingers were covered with blood. She turned around and the children screamed. Totally frightened and with blood beginning to gush from her face, she turned away from the children and ran down the stairs.

"I remember shouting over and over, 'Carl, Carl where are you? Please help me.' It seemed like forever before he heard me and came running into the hall.

The first thing he said was, 'Oh, my God!' He wasn't swearing; it was a prayer." Because there was so much blood, Carl led her out of the house and onto the front lawn.

"A group of teenagers from next door came running over to help. They weren't able to do much, but they were there at a time when I was afraid to be alone. While the kids stayed with me, Carl ran back inside to use the telephone. I don't think he realized how badly I was cut, because he didn't call a doctor or an ambulance. He called my mother. Mom was supposed to go to a meeting, but she had changed her mind and stayed home. Before she could come and help me, though, she needed a car and a sitter for my baby sister. She tried calling some friends and neighbors, but none of them were home.

But the Lord had special help on the way. Just when they were needed, two women and two teens from a Bible church we had attended recently stopped by to invite Mom to church. When they heard about the accident they were anxious to help. Two stayed with my baby sister, and two brought Mom to me in their car. By that time, I was in severe pain. One of the neighbors gave me a towel to put over my face. I was so frightened and hurt that I hardly knew what was happening, I saw Mom arrive with two strange women. One of them went into the house with Carl to take over my babysitting and start cleaning up. Mom and the other lady helped me into a car and drove off in the direction of the hospital. By the time we got there, the towel was soaked with blood, but none of it seemed real to me at the time."

At the hospital, Mary was taken directly to an operating room where a student intern, the only one on duty at the time, began sewing her face back together. He had to literally let drops of a deadening agent from a hypodermic needle drip into the open wound before he could do the stitching. "Mom said I looked like a split football. If that sounds awful, it was; especially when I first saw my face in a mirror. I looked terrible; two bulging black eyes, a big white gauze bandage, and beneath the bandage, thirteen black crisscross stitches, one for each year of my life."

Yet even this was evidence of God's love and concern because that intern and his stitches worked a near miracle. Several times afterward other doctors told Mary how bad she might have looked if the stitching hadn't been done just right. "When my heavenly father makes an appointment with a doctor, He makes it with the right one."

But it still wasn't over. Though she now knew that God loved her and that He had played a big part in what happened, she still hadn't met Jesus Christ personally. In fact, "I didn't know such a thing was possible. Then one evening, we visited that Bible church to say thank you to the four women who had helped us the night of my accident. There I heard about Christ's love for the first time. At the end of the sermon, there was a baptismal service. I really got excited. I'd never seen a baptism by immersion before. *Great!* I thought. *I want to be baptized that way.*

When I told my mother what I wanted to do, she said, 'Why do want to be baptized?'

I said, 'Because that's what Jesus did.'

She was delighted. 'But first,' she said, 'you have to know Jesus.' Though I wasn't aware of it, Mom had already turned her life over to Christ. She led me to a back room to talk with the pastor. He explained how I could know Christ as my personal Savior and Lord. And I prayed a prayer, together with my sister, Nancy, inviting Jesus to come into my heart and life. It was as if someone turned a light on inside me. All I wanted was to belong to Jesus Christ, to love Him, and to serve Him all my life.

Since then Mom and I had been to and talked with several plastic surgeons about removing my scar. The scar made a visible cross the length of which ran vertically down the bridge of my nose and horizontally into one of my cheeks and up into the corner of one eye. Whenever I got sunburned it turned red and was very obvious, but I finally decided to leave it as it is. The scar is my evidence that God loves me.

Today, when someone asks, 'Say, Mary, how did you get that scar?' I tell them the story of my horrible accident, but my answer doesn't stop there. I always explain how the Lord used the circumstances of that accident to reveal His love to me; a love that spared my life and my sight and led me to faith in Jesus Christ."

How about you? Where is your faith? Is it in money, or objects? Where is your hope? What can you count on in this life? Can you take it with you into the next? Jesus said, "For it is by grace you have been saved, through faith...it is the gift of God, not of works so that no one can boast" (Eph. 2:8, 9). Grace means unmerited favor, (undeserved) and faith, the evidence of things hoped for but not seen.

Mary almost bled to death. By God's grace she didn't. If you've never given your life to the Lord, don't wait for something tragic to happen to do so; you might not make it. You can pray a prayer similar to Mary's with these words: Dear Jesus, I open the door of my heart to you. Please come in, forgive my sins, and take control of my life. I receive you as my Savior and Lord and ask you to fill me with your Holy Spirit and accept me as your child.

Chapter Five

Ironic Detour

Stefanie Auslam

No, I didn't die because God wants me alive for a reason.

The reason? Sixteen-year-old Stefanie Auslam thought drinking was cool until a drunk driver crossed her path. Within seconds, the entire course of her life changed in the mangled, twisted wreckage of her car. Stefanie, a very popular young lady at Bella Vista High School was well on her way to national soccer and track championships, but also on her way into habits that were unhealthy physically, mentally, emotionally, and spiritually. Yes, God wanted her alive for a reason, and ironically, the very object steering her in the wrong direction was instrumental in bringing her back. Coincidence? Not according to Stefanie, now busy setting new track records toward preventing detours in the lives of others (especially teenagers) by sharing her story with them.

Dad transferred to Sac State from Rutgers when I was two. We lived in Carmichael, California until I was five and then moved to Fair Oaks, California where I began attending church with Mom. I really wasn't into church at that time but when I was nine, I was invited to Wolf Mountain Camp. Here six or seven of the girls began talking and sharing outside our cabin one night. Next thing we knew we were all crying and talking about church. We decided to give our hearts to the Lord, and our camp counselor prayed with us to receive Christ. Mom got me a book with Bible verses and stories I really liked, and I spent a lot of time in them.

That all changed when I got to high school. During my freshman year, I began to realize that although people liked me, I wasn't the type of person they automatically flocked to, but people were important to me. It didn't matter if they were good or bad; I just wanted to be around popular people. I was drawn to them and the things they were doing, like when my friends were drinking. It seemed fun to be with them, but then just being with them wasn't enough. I wanted to participate with them and began drinking quite a bit. It made me feel more a part of things and so mature, so cool. Though neither of my parents drank, and I knew it wasn't a good thing to do, I still drank. (I didn't realize the dangerous path I was treading on—in past generations we had a history of alcoholism on both sides of the family.)

The drinking continued into my junior year until one day during lunch when I told my friends, "I'm not going to drink any more."

They laughed and said "Oh, sure!"

They put so much pressure on me I proved them right, that I would drink again and again; I wasn't strong enough in my decision not to drink again. Two weeks after making that statement, I was at a party. Dana, my high school intern, lived across the street. When her brother saw I was drunk, he thought it was very funny and got her to come over. When she said, "You're not driving home. I will drive you home,"

I was very embarrassed. I said, "No, I'm OK." But she wouldn't let me and if she wasn't there, I would have driven home drunk.

Ironically, just two weeks later (when I wasn't drinking), I was hit by a drunk driver. I'd told Mom earlier that evening that I'd pick up my sister, Carrie, from soccer practice since I had to return a movie I'd rented anyway. As Carrie and I were heading toward the video store, a pick-up truck crossed three lanes of traffic and hit us head-on. Carrie was trapped in the car and I was pinned by the steering wheel. Carrie thought I was dead; she couldn't get out and became hysterical. By the time someone came to help, sirens were heard and the drunk had taken off; he knew he was in trouble. Carrie was taken to one hospital and I to another. Mom went with me and Dad went with Carrie. I had surgeries for hours and was in a coma for three and one-half weeks. They gave me a tracheotomy and shaved the left side of my head where they placed a bolt to measure the pressure on my brain; if it swelled, I would die.

Hundreds of people filled the Med Center, including many, many kids, so the hospital called and asked Bella Vista High to please not let so many kids come. They said kids weren't being given permission, "They were cutting classes just to get to the hospital."

When I became conscious, I knew I'd been in a car accident, but it was like a dream—like, *I'm in a car accident but I don't care, everything will be normal tomorrow.* When I was out of the coma completely (when I could raise one finger), they removed my trach and transferred me to Mercy General. At Mercy I took a lot of anti-seizure medication to relieve my hallucinations. One time I imagined I was having a party in my room and looked out my window. I saw my car out there but was drunk and so called my mom. The dream was so real the nurse came in. She knew something was wrong when I kept saying, "I have to call my mom."

The nurse said, "Well, it's midnight."

But I called Mom anyway because she'd always told me, "If you are ever drunk, just call me." So I called her and said, "Mom, don't be mad, but I'm in the hospital, I can't walk, and I'm drunk. Can you come and pick me up?"

And Mom would say, "Stefanie, go back to sleep." I was scared because I knew Mom wasn't coming for me and I didn't understand why not. But this was all part of the dream, except for the phone call, that was real.

Learning to walk was really difficult because my attitude was all messed up. In the past I'd gotten a big head; I thought I was really something and so when they tried to teach me, I kept thinking *I'm a national soccer player and sprinter, I don't have to learn how to walk* and I created a lot of problems. I'd wanted scholarships in both soccer and track. I'd wanted to go to the Olympics; then this happened. The way I see it is that it was God. He saw what I was doing – so stupid of me to go and drink all the time. And it's true. I can't do sprints anymore. I could have and really wanted to, but I didn't die!

Friends kept coming to the hospital. They prayed and read with me and brought me back really close to the Lord. I'd talk to my nurses and ask them, "Do you know why I'm alive and why I didn't die?"

And they'd say, "No, I guess you were lucky."

And I'd say, "No, I didn't die because Jesus wants me alive for a reason." Then I'd tell them they ought to become Christians too. Hundreds of Christians kept praying for me. I was told some fifty to seventy people made a circle in the hospital lobby and that there was also a big circle of kids in the school library that prayed for me. Nurses told my mom that this accident turned out to be something good because all the Christian kids at school came out of the woodwork and let it be known they were Christians.

Two weeks before Christmas I went home, and when I began attending school part time, people swarmed around me. I was the girl who was in a coma a couple of months ago. I was the girl who was supposed to die. Everyone wanted to talk to me and I was even chosen Junior Prom Queen. No small amount of attention and glamour came my way, but the best part was that my friends had stopped drinking. The rest of my junior year was great but once again, I began ignoring God; He answered all our prayers and did a miracle in my life, but all I was interested in was the boy I'd met just prior to my accident, my friends, and being Junior Prom Queen. Why is it we wait till something goes wrong before we seek Him?

When my senior year began, everyone forgot about me. Nobody paid attention to me nor seemed to remember what I'd been through. Then

Ironic Detour

I developed trouble breathing because of the scar tissue left on my vocal cords. In order to repair the damage I had to have more surgeries and ended up with another trach in January of this year. I became very sad and depressed especially with that trach in my throat. It's amazing how something like that can make you feel so subnormal. I'd forgotten the doctor's advice that I'd have times of depression and other side effects from the accident and coma, and I did everything I could to change myself. I bleached my hair, talked different, acted different, etc., all because I wasn't happy with the person I was. When the trach finally did come out (and stayed out), a new color came to my face, and I had energy and wasn't embarrassed anymore. So, now that things are good again, I'm not turning my back on God. He's part of my life and I've learned you can't just be a Christian when you want to be. You should always be ready to stand up for your faith by your walk and talk so people can see what it means.

In the middle of my senior year, I went to Washington where I met kids from all over the United States. The trach was still in my throat and when I told them what happened, some of them said, "Oh my gosh, my church prayed for you." I was finding people in other states who prayed for me that I didn't even know about, so I thank God for that trach. If it hadn't been there, they wouldn't have asked me to share about what God did for me. "In all things God works for the good of those who love Him, who have been called according to his purpose" (Rom. 8:28).

And I want to keep sharing. For example, during the month of March, my friend and I saw a sheriff who had pulled over a drunk driver. He said I could talk to him. I told him how a drunk driver almost ended my life and asked why he didn't order a Coke or something else.

He said, "The other guys would think I'm a wimp."

I told him to think about other people more because we needed to stop this. I shared about my pain and the suffering my parents and I went through.

He said he understood and that if it had happened to his son, he would've gone crazy.

When I asked the sheriff if I could talk to other drunk drivers, he said, "Just drive around Saturday nights and look for the ones that have been pulled over."

I really would like to be used to make a difference and also to be used as a witness for the Lord because you can't do it without Him.

Can you do it without Him? If Stefanie had died, she would've been in heaven because she knew Christ as her Savior when the accident happened, but what about you? Would you have been there? Stefanie believes God spared her so she could tell you about this opportunity for a new life. She'd advise you not to be filled with the spirits of alcohol (or anything else) but to be filled with the Spirit of life, Jesus Christ. You don't know if you'll see tomorrow; neither did Stefanie. Do you dare take a chance and wait? Are you heading for a detour? Jesus said, "I am the way, and the truth, and the life. No one comes to the Father except through Me" (John 14:6). Will you invite Him in and give him control of the wheel of your life? He's the only one who can steer you in the right direction, or would you rather continue to turn from one destructive detour to another until you wind up on a dead end street from which there is no return?

Jesus said, "There is none righteous, not even one" (Rom. 3:10) and "All have sinned and fall short of the glory of God" (Rom. 3:23). "For the wages of sin is death, but the gift of God is eternal life in Christ Jesus" (Rom. 6:23). This life is in His Son and it's free because He paid your way at the Cross. Jesus said, "I stand at the door and knock, if anyone hears my voice and opens the door, I will come in" (Rev. 3:20). "God has given us eternal life, and this life is in his son. He who has the Son has life; he who does not have the Son of God does not have life" (1 John 5:12).

If you would like to become a Christian, ask the Lord to forgive your sins and by faith invite Him to come into your heart and take control. You can use your own words or the following prayer: Dear Jesus, I open the door of my heart to you. Please come in, forgive my sins, and take control of my life. I receive you as my Savior and Lord and ask you to fill me with your Holy Spirit and accept me as your child.

Chapter Six

Sudden Eclipse

I'll take her back anyway you want to give her back.

Dave Auslam was willing to accept his daughter no matter what condition she was in.

※

Hour-long minutes ticked away mercilessly before we got any word at UCD Med Center and, even then, the news about our sixteen-year-old daughter was devastating. As we sat in the ICU, disbelief sliced through the already stunned and silent chambers of our hearts. Just a few hours earlier, she had happily hopped into her car saying, "I'll pick up Carrie from soccer practice for you Mom; I've got to return a video anyway."

Stefanie, our oldest daughter, was a ceaseless powerhouse of energy and an all-star soccer player who participated in national championships. She was also one of the fastest track athletes in the county and took great pride in her ability to run. We wondered how this would affect her if she survived.

This sudden and ominous shadow in our lives gave me plenty of time to think in the days, weeks, and months that followed; time to thank God I was a Christian; time to think about Stefanie, the drunk driver, my family, my life; time to remember the Ozark Mountains where I was born and my parents who, though they were never church-goers, never denied me the opportunity of going; and time to remember Grandmother who had come from a family of circuit riders (men who carried the Gospel from cabin to cabin and preached in our tiny churches). She never ceased telling us about Jesus. She'd read the Bible every day and though she wasn't perfect, was an example to us. I realize now her influence was what compelled me to put some faith behind my beliefs while I was just a youngster in junior high, and when our youth director extended an invitation to receive Christ, I couldn't ignore the tugging in my heart and asked Jesus to come and live in my heart, forgive my sins, and take charge of my life. It was then my love for God ignited and rapidly ushered me to the head of my Sunday school class, but my enthusiasm only lasted until high school. Here, in my junior year it gave way under heavy peer pressure and raced recklessly through parties, girls, and all kinds of friends; I had put God on a shelf. From time to time I'd hear a hymn or Billy Graham would catch my eye for a few minutes on TV, but basically, I just never had time for God anymore. "No one can serve two masters. Either he will hate the one and love the other, or he will be devoted to the one and despise the other" (Matt. 6:24).

After one and one-half years in the Army, I married Lu. Like me, she sensed a real need and desire for church but still we never seemed to find time for God. After my discharge we moved to Sacramento and then to New Jersey where I graduated from Rutgers University. After that, we returned to Sacramento. Stefanie was now a year old. Five months later, her sister, Carrie, was born. With two children, we were convinced it was time for us to attend church regularly. We found a good church in Fair Oaks, California, and became members. I developed a strong desire to study the Bible, which sent me searching from one study to another; I wanted one really committed to studying God's Word. Then about seven years ago, in 1983, I was invited to meet with a large group of men to learn about a new study just starting. When the leader of this group said it was time to pray, he got on his knees and, to my surprise, in the middle of some thirty to forty men from many different churches, prayed aloud that the men of Sacramento would become committed to studying the Bible, there would be a revival, that men would start leading their families, loving their wives, and living as Christ wanted them to live. And that was the beginning of Men's Bible Study Fellowship (MBSF) in Sacramento. In time I learned enough to become a substitute teacher and not long after that, in September 1988, was asked to consider being a regular teacher/leader the following year.

About a month later, (the night of October 4, 1988) as Lu and I were sitting in the family room talking about this new responsibility, the phone rang. A woman's voice said, "Your children were in an automobile accident." We immediately went to our knees and asked God to protect them and to give us strength to endure what we were about to see. We sped to the scene and there it was—Stefanie's smashed and mangled car, ambulance and police lights, the glass and the pick-up truck. Our girls were lying on stretchers. Stefanie was unconscious but Carrie was awake. We were told a drunk driver in a pick-up had crossed three lanes of traffic at more than sixty miles an hour and hit Stefanie's car head-on after which he fled, leaving the two girls to die.

Lu went over to Stefanie, and I went to Carrie who said, "I don't feel too good, but I think I'm alright. Stefanie isn't, go check on her."

I went over to one of the emergency workers and said, "What's wrong with my daughter?"

He said, "Not good—we think she's alive but we don't know for how long."

Life Flight couldn't get a helicopter for her because it was already in use and so she had to go to the hospital by ambulance.

"Will she live?" I asked.

"I don't think so, but we won't know until we get her to the Med Center."

I remember dropping to my knees right there on top of the glass in the middle of the street and praying, "She's Yours anyway, You created her, but You know how much I love her." I asked God to protect her and that if He took her, I'd understand, but that, "I'll take her back anyway You want to give her back." I wanted her and would accept her no matter what condition she was in. Lu repeated that prayer with me again later.

It was a tough commitment and difficult for us to keep in the months that followed, but as Stefanie lay in a coma for the next three and one-half weeks, our church began pouring their love over us. From that very first night in the ICU as we waited for x-ray results, there were four or five of them with us praying for answers. As we rose from our knees, the technician came in with the x-rays and a picture of her brain. He pointed to lesions on the right side and said she had head injuries and trauma and it appeared she would live but only as a vegetable. Further, that we could count on her never being able to walk again. A resuscitator was placed in her throat and, not long after that, a tracheotomy was performed so she could breathe easier.

There were tubes all over Stefanie's body trying to keep her alive. Her heartbeat ran between 170 to 190 beats per minute for one and one-half days. You could tell her body was totally out of control;

everything was shut down. The cardiologist said she had a very large heart because she was an athlete and that's why it was beating so fast.

While she was in intensive care, only family members could be in that area but different friends from church stayed twenty-four hours a day. And, their love kept coming—it came in casseroles, in taking care of the house, and other things; I don't think Lu cooked a meal for almost two and one-half months. We began a program of living at the hospital, but the doctors didn't want us staying all night. They'd send us home while friends stayed in the waiting room to bring us news and to pray for her. Love kept pouring from every direction. Can you imagine about fifty to seventy men and women standing in the waiting room of the Med Center, hand-in-hand, praying out loud for the life of our daughter? And that's not counting the now almost two hundred members of MBSF with a representation of over seventy churches in Sacramento who daily fasted and prayed for her recovery. "If my people who are called by my name, will humble themselves and pray, and seek my face and turn from their wicked ways, then I will hear from heaven and will forgive their sin and will heal their land" (2 Chron. 7:14).

In addition to prayer, we read the Gospels and Psalms to her each day until she was moved out of intensive care with all its tubes, bells, and whistles; she was still in a coma but apparently improving. In acute care she could have visitors, and people from our church would come, pray, and even sing to her. Then one morning as we were just getting up, we got a call that Stefanie had opened her eyes, just a flicker, but she had opened her eyes. We were told she may open them completely, and she may not. Eventually, she did, but she still had no movement on her left side whatsoever. We were told it would probably never move. It did, and prayers kept coming! We were told she will never speak normally again, prayers kept coming, and she did! "Pray continually...give thanks in all circumstances" (1Thess. 5:17, 18).

Stefanie is an amazing young lady; she's got so much determination that she almost killed herself as she got out of bed one night and tried to walk out of the hospital so they gave her a bed on the floor. We'd go in every day to pray with her and she'd say, "Dad, don't forget to read to me tonight." When we couldn't, some other loving friend was there to read the Bible and pray with her. "Do not let this book of the law depart from your mouth; meditate on it day and night, so that you may be careful to do everything written in it. Then you will be prosperous and successful" (Josh. 1:8).

We were told she'd have to live in a rehab center in the Bay area for a while but, on December 16, about two and one-half months after the accident, she came home instead. The doctors said, "We've never seen anything like this."

And we'd say, "Well, you've never seen anything like our God," and the prayers continued as she learned to walk, talk normally, brush her teeth, and do all those things again.

In February of 1991 she resumed track practice at Bella Vista and shortly after that took a trip to Washington with forty-five other students to witness a debate before Congress as to whether or not drunk drivers should be tested for drug abuse. She still had a trach in her throat but she went anyway. They met with about two hundred other kids from all over the United States and after the debate, split up into smaller groups on the Senate floor for a discussion. And there, among all those kids, Stefanie shared her story. Three girls came up from behind as they were leaving and tapped her on the shoulder. They said, "Stefanie, we know you."

"You know me?" she asked.

"Yes," they said, "because while you were in the hospital in a coma, we were praying for you."

Prayer is powerful; it changes things and crosses incredible boundaries. It changed the way I felt toward the drunk driver. As a natural man, I wanted to strangle him, but God didn't allow me to expend any energy that way. He never allowed me to have any hatred or resentment towards him, and when we went to the courtroom and publicly forgave him, we knew it had to be because of God's supernatural power. He was sentenced to eight years but he needed to seek God's forgiveness more than ours, and we encouraged him to do that while he was in prison.

It's been almost two years since the accident and except for the scar where her trach was, you couldn't tell what happened. A number of specialists told us

Stefanie's recovery was miraculous. And so it was. God decided to heal her for a very definite purpose; we believe she realized that and is using her time and energy to keep other kids and their families from a sudden eclipse.

How about you? Dave Auslam was willing to accept his daughter no matter what condition she was left in. Did you know that God loves you even more? Where are you in relation to the Lord? If you were to experience a "sudden eclipse," would you be ready to meet Him? Wouldn't you like to remove the eclipse of sin separating you from God, that black ominous shadow blocking the Sonlight of His love? Jesus, the light of the world, can remove it forever, right now!

Or, do you dare wait and chance a total eclipse (death) from which there is no way back? After death your mouth is shut. "For with your heart you believe and are justified, and it is with your mouth that you confess and are saved" (Rom. 10:10). What would you say to God if He asked you, "Why should I let you into my heaven?" Is there anything He doesn't already have that you could offer Him for your life?

The spiritual cancer of sin will not be cured by your good deeds anymore than physical cancer would, Jesus said, "I am the resurrection and the life, He who believes in Me shall live even if he dies" (John 11:25). He is the light of the World. In Him there is no darkness. He is the way through the darkness, through the shadows in your life.

If you want to remove the eclipse of sins blocking you from the Sonlight and the assurance of eternal life, pray the following prayer to receive Christ into your heart: Dear Jesus, Thank you for the gift of eternal life. I know I am a sinner and that I cannot save myself. I believe You are the Son of God and that You died for my sins and rose again from the dead. I accept You now as my Savior and Lord. Please come into my heart, receive me as your child and fill me with Your Holy Spirit.

CHAPTER SEVEN

PRESIDENT FERDINAND E. MARCOS

FERDINAND E. MARCOS

What happened July 23, 1989?
See page 9

Do you know what God is doing? I thought I did. The surprises in this story are astounding. They emphasize God's awesome compassion, humor, integrity, loyalty, faithfulness, and forgiveness. You'll see how He changed every one of our plans to conform to His will in bringing about the purpose He wants made manifest. I find humor in the fact that He really will use some of the foolish things of this world to confound the wise, thereby making his awesomeness even more awesome.

Accordingly...this story is dedicated to, and in the name of the Lord, Jesus Christ. To Him be the glory!

Important facts:

a. In May 1986 I was convicted to leave my job and start Christian Courier Ministries as an outreach to Sacramento.

b. As the outreach ministry grew, Dale and Kay Ferranto (a couple in my church) felt it was God's will for them to send me and my daughter, Heather, to Urbana '87, a missions conference held in Illinois every three years during the month of December.

c. Urbana '87 led to my invitation to Leadership '88 held in Washington DC that July. Here I met my predestined roommate, Claire Ngata of Honolulu. It was during this '88 conference that we heard about the Lausanne II Congress on World Evangelism scheduled to be held in Singapore, July 11-21, 1989. Thousands wanted to go but we were told attendance was by invitation only and only four hundred would be invited from the United States. Thus, my parting comments to Claire were, "Well, Claire, I don't expect to get to Lausanne, but I know I'll see you again; I know God brought us together for a definite reason."

d. Just before we left, the location for Lausanne II was suddenly changed from Singapore to Manila, Philippines. This change is very significant and strategic to the events that follow because exactly one year later (in July of 1989) Claire and I did meet again. God's timing is unfathomable!

Matthew 28:19, "Go, therefore and make disciples of all nations."

Background information:

I'd prayed for a short-term mission for three years and particularly for a trip to Haiti. Instead, I got an invitation to Lausanne II Congress, Philippines. "This is great, Lord," I said, "but not what asked for, and since you didn't provide the money for Haiti, how can I even think of going to Lausanne?" Three weeks later, in March 1989, my short-term mission became a reality. When? Incredibly just two weeks prior to the Congress. Where? Incredibly, not Haiti but Tarlac, just two hours north of Manila where Lausanne II was to be held. Not only did I have an invitation to Lausanne, but my three-year prayer was answered. I got what I wanted plus a bonus.

At this point I thought I had God figured out, but He wasn't finished yet. Three months later, my pastor's secretary, Marion Dakin, jokingly said, "You ought to stop in Honolulu on your way back and see Marcos."

"Who's Marcos?" I said, to her disbelief. After updating me on this former Filipino President, I said, "Well, I'll just do that if I get there."

Marion laughed, "I doubt it," she said. "He's critically ill and so well guarded, nobody's able to get in to see him."

"But Marion" I said rather flippantly, "You know nothing's impossible to God."

"Yes, I know," she chuckled, "but could you get in to see the President of the United States?"

"Well, not likely," I said heading out of the room. But, just before I closed the door, I stuck my head back in and said, "If Jesus wants me there, I'll be there."

"Oh, get out!" she gestured, laughing.

I gave it no further thought but night after night thereafter I was plagued with Marcos' name and couldn't sleep. Night after night I was reminded, *Marcos needs Me. He's asking for Me and is crying to Me for help.*

Finally, I said, "OK, Lord, if you want me to see Marcos, You arrange it and I'll go!" I was then reminded, *Faith without works is dead,* so I called Wilcox Travel only to hear what I already knew;

everyone wants a stopover in Honolulu. There's a mile-long list both before and after the Lausanne Congress." But they didn't discourage me and suggested my checking with Northwest Airlines myself. I told Northwest I needed to visit a very critically ill person and this was my only opportunity to do so. (I didn't dare tell them who that ill person was.) Even though I called them almost every day, they never complained, and after a few days I was wait-listed on one, two, three, and then five flights. They said I was top priority and would have the very first cancellation that came in. I'd never been top priority on anything in my life, and considering there were over a thousand on the waiting list, this was not as encouraging as it sounded. It was even less so when, on June 28, 1989 (my departure date) there were still no openings. Northwest said, "Be sure to let us know where to reach you when you get to the Philippines."

When I get there! I almost didn't. I was hastily shuffled onto a Delta Flight to LA after USAIR #2830 out of Sacramento was suddenly cancelled. Part of my luggage was on its way to Manila and part of it on USAIR, Delta, or Northwest. After arriving in LA and hiking from one terminal to another in search of my luggage, I was already exhausted when my missionary teammates (Nick, Chris and Job Vogt, and Todd Noonan of Christian Team Ministries) and I boarded Northwest #23 for Manila. After fifteen hours (on a flight which, unknown to us, lost some of its fuselage on take-off), many of the passengers were ready to abandon ship. They needed relief from their "seat calluses" and the numerous children and babies on board who had long before sought the aisles as a refuge from boredom.

To our surprise, we did abandon ship. As we landed in Korea to deplane passengers bound for Seoul, we almost crashed. We were told there was major damage to our plane with a huge hole in one tire and a bent axle, not to mention the missing fuselage. We thanked God for our miraculous landing. However, the grueling forty-minute trip to the Ambassador Hotel on a hot sticky night after hours of first processing through customs, left no small impact on the three hundred or so passengers now stranded in a foreign country without their luggage. (Picture living in the same clothes for three straight days!)

During our second day, a riot broke out in front of the hotel between the military, local police, and North Korean students. Firebombs, tear gas, and rocks went flying through the air and two of our hotel windows were blown out. Many of the passengers panicked, but through it all, several found Christ as their Savior.

As we worked together with other missionaries and pastors on board to comfort those who were frightened, angry, and distressed, we discovered a widow whose husband had been killed in Manila a week earlier and a woman having a heart attack. We prayed with them and both accepted Christ. The Lord made His presence known every step of the way. We finally made it to Manila where we spent two weeks with Pastor Federico Bong Manuel, Jr. ministering in the province of Tarlac.

It was at the end of these two weeks that I finally got a call from a travel agent for Northwest Airlines saying she "may have a ticket for me to go to Honolulu." The catch was that I had to give up my return ticket to the United States before she could give me the one to Honolulu. My teammates went on to New Zealand and I to the Lausanne Congress where I was to meet this agent at a local restaurant in Manila. Here I would give her my ticket and then had to trust her to come back the next day and give me the one for Honolulu. I knew that if I got that ticket it would be a miracle. Would she come back? She did. When that ticket was placed in my hands, I knew I would get to see Marcos.

The Congress ended on July 21; I had to leave July 20 (one day early) in order to be able to use this miraculous ticket. The night before my departure a typhoon struck. We had to be at the airport four or five hours earlier. The plane struggled against the monstrous winds and almost didn't get off the ground. We heard later that the next plane that came in crashed across the runway and the airport was shut down. This was only one of many obstacles the enemy used to try to prevent God's plan from succeeding, but nothing can withstand the unfathomable power of the Spirit of the Lord.

Nobody Gets to See President Marcos

This incredible story is written with the permission of Irene Araneta (Marcos' daughter) whom I met in St. Francis Hospital in Honolulu, on July 23, 1989, three days after leaving the Lausanne Congress.

※

"Is this a dream?" I said to my friend, Claire Ngata, as we left the hospital? No, it's not a dream," I said, answering my own question. "But, it must be a dream. Things like this don't happen." Claire let me ramble on; she too, was sensing the awesomeness of what God had just done. "The impact is just now hitting me," I continued. "Maybe I'm going into shock...maybe I should laugh...or cry, or... No, I've already cried. Claire, do you feel like I do?"

"Yes," she said, "It's pretty incredible, isn't it. When you first came, Catherine, I really didn't think you'd get in to see Marcos. It seemed so impossible, especially after you got turned down so many times."

"Well, Jesus knew I couldn't have done it without you Claire. Do you remember what I said a year ago at the Leadership '88 conference in Washington, D.C., about how I knew the Lord brought us together for a reason but I didn't know the reason?

"That's right!" Claire almost shouted. "I do now," she said. "I'd forgotten about that."

"Claire, it's unfathomable, but God planned this over a year ago! I wonder what we'd have done, had we known then what we'd be doing today," I said, as I continued to ramble. "Me and you—nobodies in the eyes of the world; are we really here? We are, aren't we? And why me; why you? Why not a pastor or someone famous?"

"I don't know," Claire said, "His ways are not our ways." (But we knew three months later, that it was so that His unfathomable power to do the impossible would be made manifest)

No one, absolutely no one, except immediate family got in to see Marcos; his faithful and committed twenty-four-hour-a-day guards made sure of that. But then, God opened doors and there we were "ordinary little lizards" like those mentioned at the Lausanne II Congress. "It's actually sort of humorous, Claire. They said nobody gets to see Marcos. Well, in the eyes of the world we really are nobodies and so they were right because a nobody/somebody got to see Marcos." Nothing is impossible to God but this was the first time we experienced the magnitude of that biblical truth.

"I was often told how foolish I was to even consider getting a stopover in Honolulu after the Manila Congress because of the mile-long waiting list and hundreds of people ahead of me and even more foolish to think I could get into the ICU."

"You're right," said Claire, "I, too, thought it was pretty hopeless and was shocked when you called to say you'd gotten on a flight."

My thoughts went back over the last two days. I'd arrived in Honolulu on the evening of July 20. As I bent down to pick up my suitcase, a knife-like pain shot through my back; I couldn't straighten up! That evening and almost all day the twenty-first was spent in bed at Claire's home covered in an intensive blanket of prayer and praise by her body of believers.

It was Saturday, July 22, 1989 when we made our first visit to St. Francis Hospital where Marcos was in the ICU. The receptionist's smile disappeared at the mere mention of Marcos' name. "You'll have to talk to that man over there!" she said.

"That man," was Rex, one of Marcos' entourage. "We'd like to see Mr. Marcos," I began.

"Nobody gets to see Marcos!" Rex said.

"But," I continued, "I've come a very long way and I know it's God's will for me to see him. I've a message he needs to hear; he's been crying out to God for help."

"Nobody gets to see Marcos," he firmly repeated.

"Well, I know he can't have a lot of visitors, but it is important that I see him; I've come a very long way from Sacramento, California. Is there anyone I can talk to?"

"He's in intensive care and only immediate family can see him. I can't even get in and I'm family."

"Oh, are you a brother or uncle?" Claire asked.

"No, I'm part of the entourage—that's family."

"I'm sorry you haven't been able to see him," I said sorrowfully. "I know that must be difficult for you, but could you tell me how I might talk to the doctor to find out what's happening now?"

"It won't do you any good," Rex said. "You won't be able to see him, but if you want to talk to the doctor, you can try."

"Where is he?"

"Second floor," he said, pointing to the elevator.

Two men sat just outside the elevator doors. We walked past them and turned the corner to our left to the ICU waiting room. One door of the ICU was open. As we peeked in and I said, "I don't know where to go," the two men we'd just passed approached us to ask if they could help. Once again, smiles disappeared at the mention of Marcos' name.

The tallest one, Pascua, said, "Nobody gets to see Marcos." (Here we go again, I thought, but God reminded me they were just doing their job and doing it very well.) I repeated my story and pleaded with Pascua about how God wanted me there, how He opened special doors for my plane ticket, and provided funds I didn't have, etc.

"Could you please see if the doctor would talk to us even a few minutes?"

He went inside and when he returned, said, "I'm sorry; the doctor said no one can see Marcos. They are busy with him now. Besides, you'd have to get permission from the First Lady to see him."

"Will she be here today?"

"She was here this morning and she usually only comes once a day," he said. "Can we wait? Is it possible she might return?"

"You can wait, but I think you're wasting your time."

After assuring us he'd send word if she came in, we went back downstairs. When we told Rex what happened; his smile reminded us of what he'd said, "It won't do you any good to go up there." We sat and prayed and read our Bibles. Other guards came and went. We could see Rex talking to them and saw them looking at us.

"Maybe they think we're spies or something," I said to Claire.

She laughed, "Oh, Catherine, I think you're letting your imagination get the best of you."

After two hours, we decided it was useless to wait. "I'll go upstairs to let Pascua know we're leaving." I asked Pascua if he could please call Mrs. Marcos to let her know we were there, and then I felt compelled to ask for her phone number. "Would you give me her number; could I call her myself?"

"Yes," he said, as I looked at him in disbelief. When I called Imelda Marcos, the "entourage," and there were several of them I went through before one of them said she couldn't speak with anyone as she was busy with attorneys.

We decided to go to dinner with a young lady from YWAM that I'd met at Lausanne II. Her family was spending a few days in Honolulu also. They prayed with Claire and me for a miracle. The next day, Sunday, a new man guarded the second floor elevator. We ignored him and walked right into the ICU unit until a nurse at the desk stopped us and said, "May I help you?

"We'd like to see Mr. Marcos," I said.

"Oh, are you family?"

"Well.... not exactly."

As usual, the smile vanished and in a not so friendly tone she said, "Wait here!" (Unknown to us at the time, we were just a few feet from Marcos' room.)

Within moments she returned with another nurse who quickly escorted us out of the unit and marched us over to the new guard, stating, "*Alex! No one is allowed to see Marcos,*" and left us in his custody. (What now, Lord?) Once more we repeated our story and pleaded with Alex for help as time was running out. He didn't know what he could do. We apologized for the trouble we caused him by going directly into the ICU unit without permission and asked if we could pray with him and he said yes.

First, I asked the Lord's forgiveness for getting these guards into trouble and then thanked Him for them and the good job they were doing in protecting their President. We then asked for His mercy and intervention in the situation because we knew it was His will for us to be there.

After prayer (to our surprise) he said, "One thing I can do is to give you Col. Art Aruiza's phone number. He is the one who could get you permission to see Marcos."

As we left, Claire said, "I can't believe you got that number; Col Aruiza is Marcos' right-hand man."

"We're not there yet," I said, but knew God didn't send me all this way for nothing.

I dialed the number.

"Who's calling?" asked a young boy. (The boy happened to be Col. Aruiza's son.)

"Alex told us to call," I said.

"Wait a minute," he said and a man got on the phone.

He asked a few questions and then said "Just a moment."

The next voice was that of Col. Art Aruiza. After telling him the whole incredible story, he said, "I believe you."

I almost choked as I said, "You do!"

"Yes, because even as you were speaking, I hold a letter in my hand from someone in another country who is telling me exactly the same thing."

"They are!" I said in disbelief.

"Yes," he said, "and there are several others from all over the world with similar messages requesting to see Marcos. The only difference between them and you is that you are here and they are not."

A chill ran down my back and in my heart I said, "Thank you Lord for giving me the faith to be foolish enough to just come and the courage to be obedient.

"And," he continued, "since you are here, I'll tell you what I'll do. I will call Dr. Zagala; she's been

Marcos' personal physician for twenty-five years and is very religious. If she believes your story, she might let you see him. Give me five minutes and I'll call you back; she may even call you herself."

Claire picked up her guitar as we sat on her living room floor, and we began singing praises and prayers to the Lord. Five minutes passed; then ten, then fifteen, then twenty. "I can't stand it any longer," I said "I've got to call back." It was now twenty minutes to five on Sunday night. I apologized to Col. Aruiza for not waiting, saying we had to go to church and I didn't know what to do.

"When do you have to leave?" he asked.

"About 5:15 P.M."

He told me to wait, saying we would hear before 5:00 P.M. At ten minutes to five the phone rang. It was Dr. Zagala. Claire prayed as I repeated the awesome miracles the Lord had done in getting me to Honolulu.

Then Dr. Zagala said, "Could you pray for him in the chapel and we could bring the message to him?"

"Yes, I could," I said, "but then he wouldn't hear my voice and wouldn't know that I actually did come all this way just because God heard his cries and wanted to help him."

"Do you have to touch him?" she said.

From within I felt compelled to say, "No, my mission is to deliver a message that God wants him to hear. The Lord told me Marcos cannot speak but that he can hear and that he has been crying out from within his spirit for help." (I didn't know Marcos' couldn't speak or why.)

"You can come," she said. (Another chill went down my back)

"When?"

"Right now."

"I'm on my way," I said as I hung up the phone, flew into my shoes, and ran out the door with Claire racing beside me toward her car. We had all we could do to stay within the speed limit as we sang, prayed, and thanked God.

At 5:10 P.M. we ran past the receptionist into the elevator, never stopping to see about guards. Alex greeted us as we got off the elevator and we'd barely caught our breath when Dr. Zagala and Irene Araneta (Marcos' daughter) arrived. The doctor had told Irene about us and she wanted to be with her father when I talked to him. Claire was not allowed in the room with me; I had to leave my purse, etc. with her, and I was given a sterile gown to put on.

As I entered the room, I saw a frail, gentle looking man with a swollen face; his eyes were closed and a trach tube was protruding from his throat. (So that's why you said he couldn't speak, Lord.) Incredibly, my fears were gone and an awesome peace surrounded me. Two attendants were adjusting some apparatus.

"When they finish, you can talk to him," Zagala said as she handed me a yellow sterile mask to wear over my mouth. There were seven people in the room, including me.

Irene went over to her father and very gently brushed the side of his left cheek with the back of her hand. "Daddy," she said with a tenderness that left me misty-eyed. "It's me, Irene, I've brought someone—there's someone here to see you."

As she stepped aside, I approached the bed and Marcos began to open his eyes. They got wider and wider and, as I began to speak, he fixed his gaze on me. I could read the question in his eyes, *Who are you?*

"Mr. Marcos," I said, "My name is Catherine, and I know the Lord Jesus must love you very much because He sent me all the way from Sacramento, California to come to see you. The airlines said there were no seats available but He got me a seat. He told me you have been crying to him for help and that even though no one else could hear you, He did. So, I'm here to let you know that He heard your prayer and has a message that will help you." (Marcos' eyes began to get watery; you could tell he was intent on my every word.)

"What I'm going to say may sound strange to you and the others, but Jesus said you would understand it completely; He wouldn't have gone to the trouble of bringing me here if you didn't. He said to remind you of when you were a little baby in your mother's womb; to remember how you were in darkness and couldn't see, but how you could move, kick, eat, breathe, and even cry. No one could see you, but He saw every move you made, and no one could hear you, but He heard every cry you uttered. He said that now, once again, you've been in a darkness where no one could hear your cries but that, just as He heard them in the darkness of the womb, He's heard them from the beginning of your inability to speak, and that's why He's convinced me to come and made a way for me to get here.

He said to remember that if you hadn't pushed your way out of the womb, you would have died in it because you no longer had any room to move. You had to push your way out of the darkness and into the light. When you did, you experienced a new freedom, saw the light, and felt the warmth of your mother's arms for the first time. Well, once again, you need to come out of darkness into light, and to feel the warmth of your heavenly Father's arms. But this time, it's in reverse.

Let me explain: You don't come into the light, the Light comes into you. 'Flesh gives birth to flesh but the Spirit gives birth to spirit' (John 3:6). Your physical birth was an exit but your spiritual birth is an entrance. The spirit of man lives on the inside where no one can see it but God. The physical birth is an exit into the world of man. The spiritual is an entrance into the world of God—the entrance of Jesus by way of the Holy Spirit coming into the heart of man." Tears were beginning to trickle down Marcos' face and I knew he was understanding.

"Jesus said to repeat again that just as He heard your cry in the womb, and just as He heard your cries for help these many months even though you were unable to speak, that if you responded to this message He is bringing you through me and if you are willing to repeat a prayer with me inviting Jesus into your heart, He would hear it and accept it and you would receive Christ as your Savior. So, if you want to receive Jesus as your Savior, Mr. Marcos, all you need to do is to pray these words that I am going to say right now…"

Instantly, and before I could say another word, Marcos smiled with a grin that stretched from ear to ear revealing the whiteness of his teeth, and tears began streaming down his face to everyone's amazement.

I said, "That smile and those tears tell me and Jesus that your answer is yes. I know He can hear you, even if we can't. Mr. Marcos, just repeat these words in your heart and you will receive and know Him as your Lord and Savior: Dear Jesus, I, Ferdinand Marcos, love you and I know that you love me. I'm a sinner, and I'm sorry for all my sins because I know You paid a terrible price for them. Please come into my heart, forgive my sins and give me eternal life as you promised in your word. I believe You died on the cross for me, was buried in my place, and rose again to eternal life, and that I, too, should I die, will rise again to have eternal life with You."

(It was now 5:30 P.M. on July 23, 1989. These may not be the exact words I prayed with Marcos, but they were very similar.)

Then I said, "President Marcos, my mission is accomplished, and I have to leave." As a very frightened look came upon his face, I said, "Don't be afraid. You may never see me again, but you don't need me because you have Jesus. I came in answer to your prayer and did what God asked me to do. I'm going to leave now as I promised to stay just a little while, but I'm going to leave my Urbana '87 Bible with you; it's a very special one. Even though it's falling apart, it will enable someone to carry out the rest of God's plan for you which is to read the book of John to you every day for seven days. I don't know why seven days but that's what I'm compelled to tell you. God may heal you and He may take you home. I only know that He will do what is best for you. Also, someone is to continue reading the Bible to you each day."

As we left the room, Dr. Zagala and Irene grabbed and hugged me; there were tears in their eyes. Dr. Zagala said this was the very first time Marcos had smiled or cried, and that this was the first visible evidence they had that he even was aware of what was going on around him. Pascua, Alex, and Claire were ecstatic when we told them what happened, and we were all rejoicing in the corridor. Before leaving, I shared with Irene how to follow up with the Bible and read to her father daily. I also left a New Testament from the Gideons, which Dr. Zagala appreciated.

Yes, Lord, "nobody" did get in to see Marcos, and I'd rather be a nobody for Christ—a little lizard that gets even into kings' palaces when you want me to, and Marcos was a king, and he is now in your palace. To You, the King of Kings, be the glory!

I found out seven years later from Marcos' daughter Irene, that she knew why the Lord had said seven days. It was Marcos' favorite number. He used it on all his license plates, etc. and they knew that I couldn't have known that, but God did, which told them that God had really sent Claire and me to see him. Marcos' died two months later, and though I was invited to the funeral, I couldn't come, but Claire was given the honor of being with the Marcos' family, his entourage, and all the dignitaries as the world watched the proceedings on TV. The Lord is so good; He remembered Claire's heartache in not being able to get into the ICU and gave her the honor of letting her have and inside seat at this spectacular time in history for her obedience of service.

Closing Editorial Comments by Catherine Lusk:

As missionary and Editor-in-Chief of the Christian Courier, it is my belief that Marcos had been in deep sorrow for several months prior to his death not only for himself and his family, but for his people. I believe he wanted to make things right in the sight of God and man but because of his critical illness, together with his inability to speak, was totally incapable of making restoration or reconciliation. Thus, he did the only thing he could; he cried out to the Lord, the only one who could see his heart and hear his cries.

Someone once said, "When your life is hanging by a thread and you've nothing left but God you suddenly discover that God is all you need." Marcos' life was hanging by a thread for some time and, because of the nature and severity of his illness, all matters whether political, financial, domestic, or legal, were taken out of his hands. Even matters concerning his physical well-being were put under the control of others. I've no doubt that Marcos received Christ during my visit to him on July 23,1989 because I believe God wouldn't go to the extreme of bringing a perfect stranger (who knew very little about Marcos at the time), and who had no money, so many miles to share the Gospel with a man who had no interest in Him. Therefore, I believe Marcos was reconciled to God through Jesus Christ two months before he died.

However, this did not solve the problem of restoration and reconciliation in the Philippines. God could have healed Marcos; He chose to take him home instead, leaving the matter of reconciliation in the hands of others. Some people were on Marcos' side and some on the Acquino's side, but who is on God's side? What does God want?'

President Marcos prayed for forgiveness and God forgave him; that opened doors of reconciliation. Unforgiveness can divide a people more than a mountain. I believe God looks at unforgiveness as uncontrollable cancer spreading unfathomable roots of bitterness, jealousy, anger, selfishness, and even greed, etc. What does God want? He certainly does not want the suffering and fighting to continue; He does not want the Philippine nation divided. He wants us all to follow Jesus' example on the Cross: "Father, forgive them..." and He leaves us with very strong advice on the matter. Matthew 6:14 says, "If you forgive men when they sin against you, your heavenly Father will also forgive you. But if you do not forgive men their sins, your Father will not forgive your sins."

In Mark 11:25, we read, "And when you stand praying, if you hold anything against anyone, forgive him, so that your Father in heaven may forgive you..." I believe that just as God brought Marcos to peace with Him, that it is His will for these Philippine families to be at peace with each other, to find forgiveness through Him for each other, and do all they can to help their people mend the wounds that have torn them apart, thereby bringing reconciliation and peace within their borders.

Chapter Eight

In My Heart Too!

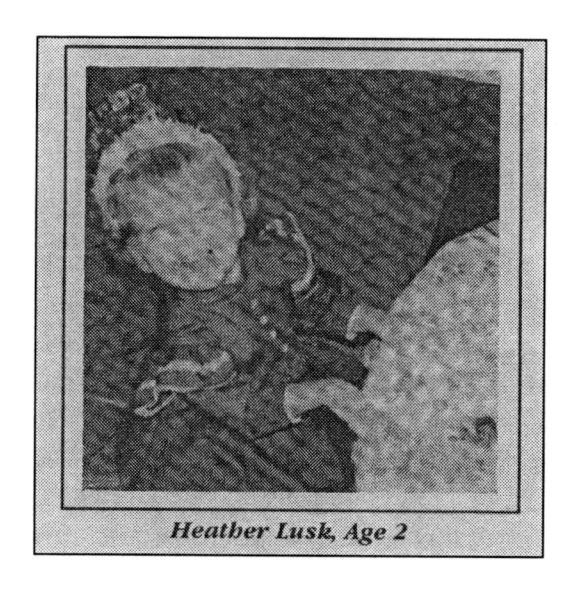

Heather Lusk, Age 2

They buried Him, but He's not dead.

Heather Lusk was just two and one-half years old, but she knew what she was talking about when she said, "They buried Him, but He's not dead."

Eternal Makeovers

Bang! went Heather's fork on the table; a judge's gavel couldn't have made a more dynamic entrance. "Mama!" she said with authority, as we stared wide-eyed and speechless. I was the first to speak after this abrupt interruption by our two and one-half year old. It was December, Dad was in Vietnam, and her sisters and I had been excitedly chatting about Christmas and the recent acceptance of Christ by some friends we'd been praying for.

"What's wrong?" I asked, thinking she was ill or something because Heather had never interrupted our conversation at dinner before.

"Mama," she repeated, "I want Jesus in my heart, too!"

I could tell by the look on her sisters' faces that they were thinking the same thing I was, *What could a two and one-half year old possibly know about Jesus?* After catching my breath at this profound statement by my baby, and before the girls could say a word, I put up my hand motioning for them to be silent and said, "Honey, that's wonderful, but you can't invite someone into your heart when you don't know who it is you're inviting in."

"I know who Jesus is," she replied very emphatically.

"You do!" I said.

"Yes!" she said.

"Well, suppose you tell me who Jesus is," I said with a wink to the girls.

In My Heart Too!

"God's Son!" she answered proudly with a smile on her face.

"Well, honey, that's right, but you need to know a bit more than that. Can you tell me something about Jesus; do you know what He did?"

"Yes," she said. "He died."

"Do you know how?" I asked, now curious to see just how much more she knew.

"The bad men put nails in His hands and feet and one man was very, very mean and stuck Jesus in the side and all Jesus' blood ran out."

At this point I had to catch my breath again, but eagerly pursued the questioning. "Do you know why He died?"

"For all the bad things people do," she answered.

"That's right, I said, totally astonished. "And, where is Jesus right now. Is He dead?"

"Oh no," she said. "They buried Him but He's not dead, He's alive and He's up in heaven with the Father."

I could go no further. I looked incredibly at this baby and said, "Honey, if you want to ask Jesus into your heart, you go right ahead and do it, but I can't do it for you. You've got to do it yourself" (I thought that if the Lord did this much in her life already, He surely would give her the words to receive Him.)

Heather leaned back in her highchair, folded her arms and looked intently up at the ceiling as if she were looking straight into heaven. Then, as if we weren't even present, she said loudly and with a pleading type of command, "Jesus, will you come into my heart too? Please?"

The girls and I sat in stunned silence waiting for what would happen next. Then, a smile slowly crowned Heather's face, igniting a twinkle in her eyes as she broke into a big grin. She next gently unfolded her arms and with her right hand and forefinger turned into her chest by her heart, she said, "Now, He's in my heart too, and He's right here, and He's never coming out." Then she laughed and clapped her hands with glee and we all rejoiced with her. She never once saw or heard the doubts that hid behind our eyes taunting, *Is this for real?*

Her sisters were seven and ten when they received Christ; it was difficult for us to believe this was possible, but the Lord quickly showed us that it was because the very next morning when Heather woke up at 5:30 A.M., she stood up, leaned over the railing (her crib was next to my bed) and said, "Good morning, Jesus; good morning, Mama, how are you today?" She'd never done that before. (We'd always taken Heather to Sunday school but thought she was playing as most two-year-olds do. We now realized she did a lot more listening and perceiving than we were aware of.)

"It's real!" I said to the girls as I shared the incident with them, but they had to hear it for themselves so they stationed themselves outside the bedroom door the next morning and listened. Sure enough, Heather got up and repeated her, "Good morning, Jesus, etc."

In My Heart Too!

When Dad came home from Vietnam almost a year later, he too, was convinced as Heather not only said good morning to Jesus but added, "Thank you Jesus for bringing my daddy home safe." But even before Daddy came home, Heather became one of the littlest evangelists ever.

I used to hear her underneath our kitchen window in Arizona talking to the little children. "Do you want to go to heaven?" she would ask.

"Yes," they would say.

"Well, you can't go to heaven unless you have Jesus in your heart."

"How do we get Jesus in our heart?"

"Kneel down and I'll tell you what to say and do." She would proceed to tell them about Jesus and what He did and then lead them in a prayer asking Him to come into their hearts, and then they would sing and dance outside that window. Was it real?

Real enough so that when one little girl went home and told her father about it, he slapped her so hard, she had five finger-marks on her face and came running to us saying "My father said I can't have Jesus in my heart and if I ever told him again that I did, he would beat me, and I can't play with you anymore." The girls cried and prayed that Jesus would help her to keep it a secret and to be obedient and pray for her father. She was convinced her daddy would one day know Jesus too.

Heather isn't a baby anymore, but we have a treasure chest of memories and stories of the awesome power of a real, living, and loving God and Father and what He can do in the life of a child who is committed to Him at an early age. Have you shared Jesus with your little ones; do they know who He is? Do they see His love in you? We praise the Lord for the love Heather still has for Him to this very day and the love she has for others to know him.

I'd like to share two more occasions in Heather's earlier years with you. At age four, a mechanic drove us home from the repair shop where we left our car. On the way, Heather looked at him and asked, "Do you know Jesus?"

I thought we'd have an accident as he hit the brakes in astonishment. "Well, uh, yes, uh, I do", he sputtered, "but do you know Jesus?" (He could not imagine a four-year-old knowing who Christ was.)

It only took a few moments for Heather to convince him. She couldn't read the Bible yet but had several verses memorized, remembered much about what she heard and was taught, and had a faith that went deeper than most adults. She could pray one-half hour or more with ease and had a real burden for those she prayed for.

Also at the age of four, while living in Omaha, Nebraska, one of her friends who was very poor didn't have a snowsuit. "Mama, could I give her one of mine?"

"Of course," I said. We had just bought Heather a new one. A short time later as we got ready to go out, Heather put on her old snowsuit and I said, "Honey, I thought you were going to give one of your snowsuits to your little friend."

In My Heart Too!

"I did, I gave her my new one," she said. And then, reading my thoughts, she added, "Aren't we supposed to give Jesus our very best?"

Tears filled my eyes with shame as I realized that my little girl was more obedient than I was. She did exactly what Jesus would have done. "Whatever you did for one of the least of these brothers of mine, you did for me" (Matt. 25:40). (I had always given my old things to the church for the poor; I never once thought about buying and donating something new.) We bought Heather another snowsuit, and her little friend got to know who Jesus was.

It would take an entire book to share all the many more wonderful events and lessons learned just because we didn't stop our children from coming to Jesus. But we want you to know also that God is definitely a "rewarder of those who diligently seek Him" (Heb. 11:5), and who "In all their ways acknowledge Him" (Prov. 3:6). God is faithful to his promises. He rewarded Heather in ways we never could have imagined. She always wanted to meet Billy Graham. Well, she not only met him but had an opportunity to work for him, eat with him, and have her picture taken with him when she was just thirteen. Thereafter, she met Joni Eareckson Tada and Sandi Patti. During her senior year at San Juan High School, her painting was chosen to hang in Crocker Art Museum for two months. She was also chosen valedictorian and shortly afterward became one of the top ten finalists in the Miss Teen of America

Scholarship Pageant held in San Luis Obispo in the summer of 1988.

And so, we encourage you to share Jesus with your children, not so they can get a lot of rewards (because Heather didn't know they were coming when she chose Jesus), but so they too will one day ask, "Mama, Daddy, I want Jesus in my heart too!"

"Let the little children come to Me, and do not hinder them, for the kingdom of God belongs to such as these" (Luke 18:16).

If you don't know Him and want to, we urge you to pray this prayer: Lord Jesus, I need You. Thank You for dying on the cross for my sins. I open the door of my life and receive You as my Savior and Lord. Thank You for forgiving my sins and giving me eternal life. Take control of the throne of my life, and make me the kind of person You want me to be.

CHAPTER NINE

HEAVEN VERSUS RICHARD CRABBE

"And then as I was asked, 'Guilty or not guilty?' I knew I would have to plead guilty."

Richard Crabbe, General Manager of The Africa Christian Press, was the firstborn son of his mother who came from a royal family. She was in line to become Queen Mother, one of the most powerful women in the traditional authority structure. Likewise, his father's family was well known. Many of them had been involved in the legal profession in Ghana and other parts of Africa. Nevertheless, Richard didn't know what it meant to be part of royalty until he stood defenseless before the King of Kings.

In Ghana, West Africa, I was enrolled in secondary school, a boarding school anyone could attend. It is the equivalent of high school in the United States. Grade school began at age six, but I started at age five because by that time I could already read the newspaper quite well. This put me a year ahead and into secondary school by age eleven. Until then, most of my childhood had been spent with an aunt and an uncle who became a Supreme Court Judge. He hoped I'd follow in his footsteps and even taught me the basics of cross-examination and public speaking. Although my aunt was a Christian and went to church, we didn't have a Christian home. I went to church occasionally, but many times I'd go to the beach with my uncle instead.

On entering secondary school, I joined a worldwide ministry of young people known as Scripture Union. My reasons were two-fold; my friends were there, and it kept me from being in the boarding house dormitory and away from supervision by the seniors. Also, it seemed to me that the good guys in the Scripture Union could protect me because I was sort of small. Our daily routine consisted of starting and ending the day with God. He was more than a "Good morning" or once-a-week kind of deal. He was made to be part of our every day life, and I began to take the Bible more seriously.

By the time I got to my third year, two significant things occurred. My mother had given her life to Christ, and my uncle became a judge in the high courts of Ghana. Mother began talking to me about giving my life to Christ but it didn't register very much because I thought I was good. I wasn't a bad guy and so felt I was OK, but one day, one of the seniors spoke to us during an evening prayer meeting. His message was based on Hebrews 9:27 which said, "It is appointed for men once to die and after this comes judgment." That got my attention. Coming from my type of background, I could easily understand what judgment meant. As he spoke, I envisioned my life and what it had been until now, and as it continued to unfold, I visualized myself in the court of heaven. I heard my case being called, "Heaven vs. Richard Crabbe." I saw God sitting on the throne and a great number of people gathered before the judgment seat. And then, as I was asked, "Guilty or not guilty?" I knew I had to plead guilty.

Thank goodness that senior didn't stop there. He went on to link the verse in Hebrews with 1 John 2:1, 2 that said, "Brethren, I am writing these things to you so that you may not sin. And, if anyone sins, we have an advocate with the Father, Jesus Christ." This caught my attention too, because in having been to the courts a number of times with my uncle, I knew only too well what advocate meant. (Once again, I envisioned a picture of myself in the court of heaven. Again, my case was called and, similarly, I heard, "Heaven vs. Richard Crabbe," but this time Jesus appeared as my advocate. He was by my side and as I was put into the witness box and asked to plead guilty or not guilty, He intervened on my behalf to say, "The Father sets him free because he is one of my own." In that instance I knew I had to ask Jesus to be my personal Savior.) And when this senior said, "If you don't have Jesus as your advocate, then why not pray and ask Him to become your personal Savior," and I did.

I simply said, "Lord, I know that I am guilty before you, I want Jesus to be my advocate to plead my case for me, and so today I turn my life over to you." Almost immediately, one very significant thing happened. My fear of death was gone. I used to be afraid of dying and now I kept thinking, "Oh, if I died today, I would be in heaven. How wonderful that would be." Before that, if I knew someone had died, I'd be too scared to even pass in front of their house believing I'd have nightmares if I did.

As I studied the Bible and other Christian books, I grew rapidly in my Christian growth. However, by the time I got to my senior year, I was overly confident and proud of my spiritual walk. Being very smug and comfortable, I slacked up in my Bible reading and prayed only occasionally. Before I knew it, I had drifted away from the Lord but was jolted out of my complacency when I failed to get into the university I wanted; my grades weren't good enough. When I decided to retake the exams the following year, I got serious with my Bible reading and got back close to God, and I made it into the university on my second try. Within the very first week, I joined University Christian Fellowship. They asked me to help with the *Fellowship Magazine* and in my senior year I became editor.

A few weeks before graduation, I accepted a position offered by the *Africa Christian Press* for one year. During my time with them, I corresponded with some young people who sent us testimonies of how God had helped them. I also received letters from others with questions about the Bible. I began to seriously consider doing this as a career, even though my original goal was to become a surgeon. The following week the board of directors offered me a permanent position if I wanted it. Because of my background in biochemistry and medicine, I struggled with that decision and asked for a month's leave of absence to think and pray about it. When I discussed it with my uncle who had raised me, his response shocked me. He fully endorsed this change in plans saying, "If God wants you to do so, go ahead." Coming from an unbeliever, this statement strongly confirmed to me that God was with me, and in October of 1979 I became a full-time employee of *Africa Christian Press*.

About three years later, on December 18, 1982, Richard married Vivian, his Ghana sweetheart. God blessed them with five lovely daughters. Shortly after their wedding the board sent him to Wheaton Graduate School to study for his Master's degree in Communication with Journalism as his major. This followed with a three month internship with David C. Cook Publishing Company after which he returned to Ghana to assume responsibility for the leadership of *Africa Christian Press* which currently publishes 110 various titles by Africans for African Christians in the seventeen English speaking countries in Africa. *ACP* also publishes in numerous other non-African languages and sends its books to the Caribbean Islands, Fiji Islands, Solomon Islands, and Papua New Guinea. The Lord continued to bless his efforts and in 1988, to his surprise, the Lausanne Committee asked him to be assistant editor of a book to be produced out of the Lausanne Congress in Manila in July 1989.

But, according to Richard, the best blessing of all was in being able to say, "Guilty, but debt paid in full by Jesus Christ."

How about you? Are you able to say that? Do you have an advocate with the Father or will you stand condemned on judgment day. If you haven't done so, and you should die today, it will be too late for an advocate. He's here now, knocking on the door of your heart saying, "I stand at the door and knock, if anyone hears my voice and opens the door, I will come in" (Rev. 3:20). If you want Jesus as your advocate, just pray the prayer that Richard prayed or use the following one: Dear Jesus, I open the door of my heart to you. Please come in, forgive my sins, and take control of my life. I receive You as my Savior and Lord and ask You to fill me with your Holy Spirit and accept me as Your child.

Then, if you stand before the judgment seat, you know your advocate will be there and you too, can say, "Guilty, but debt paid in full by Jesus Christ."

Chapter Ten

If You Don't Know, You Aren't

Dorene Walth, a pastor's wife, didn't know if she was a Christian but she wanted to find out, to know for certain.

※

Many children go to bed at night with the little prayer, "Now I lay me down to sleep," but my last thoughts often were, *God, if you're there, why don't you let my Dad die or be killed in an accident of some sort?* Being the daughter of an alcoholic, I could no longer handle the tension, troubles, and torment that accompanied his drinking. When he was sober I loved him because he was jolly and fun to be with; but when he was drunk, I hated him. So I both loved and hated him, and this ambivalence tore me apart.

Often embarrassed by Dad's conduct, I didn't enjoy inviting friends to my home. Usually there was shouting and crying that ended with Dad's leaving the house, slamming the door, and then finding a bar to sit in until it closed.

One night, at the age of twelve or thirteen, I was especially upset. I'd heard and seen about all I could stand. I went to my room and flung myself across my bed, weeping and feeling very sorry for myself, wondering why I deserved to live in such an atmosphere. After awhile, I just lay there, looking out my bedroom window. The sky was beautiful; brilliant stars winked back at me from above. It seemed they were twinkling just for me. As I continued to gaze at the beauty of the heavens, I was suddenly aware of a calming presence around me and I cried out, "God, when I marry, please give me a minister for a husband!" In my small circle of experience I had observed that most ministers and their wives appeared to have an extra dimension in their lives, which gave them a unique kind of happiness. I believed that living in a parsonage would surely give me the happiness and emotional stability I needed to keep me from the unpleasantries of life. (God heard my plea and remembered it, even though I soon forgot about it myself.)

Haphazardly, I searched for God and just hoped I was a Christian, but I wasn't sure. A few years later at a youth meeting in my church we had a question and answer time. To avoid embarrassment, the questions were written on paper; we were free to ask

If You Don't Know, You Aren't

anything about any subject. I asked, "How can one know whether or not he is a Christian?"

The pastor pondered for some time and then replied, "Well, if you don't know, then you aren't." In other words, he was telling me that I wasn't a Christian. This greatly disturbed me because I really wanted to be one. To my knowledge, the pastor did no further explaining, and I left the meeting with no assurance that I was a Christian and with no one telling me how I might become one.

I pushed these thoughts aside for several years as I channeled my energy in trying to excel scholastically and gain recognition with my peers in high school and college. I joined all the clubs and organizations I could think of—state band, state chorus, carnival queen attendant, etc. Socially I was into everything and was known as the life of the party.

At Dickinson State College I met Clarence, my husband. He was the one who let me know how I might become a Christian. He began telling me about having Jesus Christ in his life. At first it was kind of irritating and it made me uncomfortable, but as he continued to answer my questions, I finally decided that the missing element in my life was Jesus Christ. Clarence pointed out several scriptures about how I must receive Jesus—"But as many as received Him, to them He gave the right to become children of God" (John 1:12). The simplicity of inviting Jesus into my life was unbelievable, and yet this was what I wanted to do—I was so tired of running around, looking for happiness in activities. So, one night while we were together, I said in prayer to God, "Dear Lord Jesus, I need you. I open the door of my life and receive You as my Savior and Lord. Thank You for forgiving my sins. Take control of the throne of my life and make me the kind of person You want me to be."

Ever since that evening, I have felt Christ's presence in my life. Even though God answered my prayer and Clarence became a minister, I knew then that the parsonage was not the answer but the person of Jesus Christ was. The great thing was not so much the fact that I accepted what He had to offer, but that He accepted me. Jesus really changed me even gave me a new insight, acceptance, and love for my dad. Clarence's goals were to serve God the rest of his life. My decision made it easy for me to join him in his ministry of reaching others for Christ.

You can know whether or not you are a Christian. Don't waste all the years I did, waiting for someone to tell you. God says, "Ask and it will be given to you; seek and you will find, knock and the door will be opened to you" (Matt. 7:7).

Chapter Eleven

The Eleventh Hour!

I don't remember quite how I got it, but it had blood all over it, and I remember a thought or voice within me said, *'Drop it; drop it. Just do it; he won't see you.'"*

Nancy (Lusk) Barfknecht was only eleven years old when her life was almost taken from her. She knows today that it was only by the grace of God that she is here to share her story (together with some *highlighted* input from her mother Kaitee).

❈

It was Mother's Day, but there was still snow on the ground at Kincheloe Air Force Base, Michigan, where we lived. I vividly remember wearing my favorite purple dress, white sash, and shoes. This was a very special occasion. I was just ten and my mother, my sister Mary, and I were to be baptized. (Mom had accepted Christ just a few months earlier.) I thought it was funny when Mom wanted us to wear bathing caps so our hair wouldn't get wet because we were going out to dinner afterward. (I didn't pay attention to my unbaptized head until many years later.)

Happy can only barely touch the surface of how I felt. It was just two weeks earlier I had prayed to ask Jesus into my heart and received Him as my personal Savior. How can I describe the love I felt? I couldn't. Just to know that I was so very special; that He wanted me for His very own and wanted to live in my heart, was amazing, but I was so young. I didn't realize or even give thought to the fact that anything bad could happen to me and especially not the evil that awaited me in Arizona.

We were a military family, and we lived on base where we were protected and sheltered most of the time. Not only that, Mom was very strict about movies, acquaintances, and the activities we attended. We never ever talked about drugs, sex, crime, etc. or watched anything on TV even remotely close.

Not long after we were baptized, Dad got orders to go to Vietnam, and we were invited by Mom's friend Aunt Susie to come live in the new home she was building in Glendale, Arizona. It was July of 1971 when we made the move. My eighty-year-old grandmother moved with us. There were three bedrooms, Grandma had one by herself, my sister Mary (who was three years older than me) and I shared another, and Mom and my baby sister Heather (who just turned two) slept in the master bedroom. Dad was only with us for a couple of days before he had to leave. We were left with the entire job of unpacking. It was a very new housing development. There were only three to four houses that had people living in them. Everything was new. We loved the clubhouse where we could go play and swim, and it was fairly close to our house.

There were a lot of construction workers around, some seemed sort of crude and others were real nice. I remember Mom complaining to the builders and owners of the complex about our side door not locking properly. They said they would get around to fixing it. Our neighbors had similar problems, but they didn't think it was a major priority. Besides, we had a cop for a neighbor who lived close by. That gave us a false sense of security, especially at night, as there were hardly any lights, sidewalks, or finished streets in the area. What we didn't know (and no one told us) was that there was a drug addict/rapist operating in our vicinity. Unknown to us, the police were on a twenty-four hour alert. They either didn't want to alarm us or they thought we already knew.

Shortly after Dad left, we decided to visit my dad's parents who lived in Sonora, California. Incredibly, on the way there, all three of us – Mary, Heather, and I – came down with extremely high fevers. In addition, by the time Mom got us to a hospital some distance away from the grandparents, Heather also had pneumonia. They did three emergency tonsillectomies. Heather stopped breathing that night and almost died. I now began to realize that having and knowing Christ as your Savior doesn't mean that you never get sick. But it also showed me the miraculous power of an awesome Father who said, "I will never leave you nor forsake you," and will come to the rescue even in the eleventh hour. I didn't know then the impact those words would have on my life, nor how quickly they would apply not only to Heather, but to me and the rest of my family.

Well, tonsillectomies, etc. all behind us, we returned to Arizona looking forward to a fun-filled rest of the summer before school time. I don't recall exactly what night it was, perhaps some time in August (around the time of my birthday) as I had just turned 11, but we all got to bed late after watching a movie on TV. I was exhausted and fell into a deep sleep.

The children and their grandmother were tucked away for the night as I crawled into bed. The drapes in front of the master bedroom glass doors were open, and I remember looking out onto what seemed a beautiful full moon night. I could see the skyline of the new buildings that were going up, and then I realized that anyone out there could see me but I couldn't see them (even with a full moon) unless they were right on the patio outside my bedroom door. It was about 1:00 A.M. when I shut the drapes and drifted off to sleep.

A couple of hours later (about 3:00 A.M.), I heard a voice on my patio and someone saying "Come on. Come

The Eleventh Hour!

on!" and there was something being dragged across the patio floor. I was very groggy and thought someone must be out walking their dog in the moonlight, and fell back asleep.

Moments later, Mary came running into the room saying, "Mom, Mom, I heard a scream and Nancy's not in her bed."

"Oh, you must be dreaming," I said as I followed her back to her room. But, to my horror, she was not. There on the floor beside Mary's bed lay two burned matchsticks and a very strange odor permeated the room. (We found out later that it was marijuana.) Nancy who slept on the far side of the room was gone! Mary began to cry hysterically, and I remember shouting, "Don't cry. Call the police!" as I ran into the bathroom. Without thinking I put on a robe, and as I searched for a flashlight, noticed our sliding glass door next to the kitchen was open.

I ran outside in search of Nancy. I couldn't see or hear anyone. As I walked toward the clubhouse, I noticed a white car parked in front of it. I watched it for a while. It didn't move. At first I thought maybe I should check it out but then I told myself someone left it there overnight and continued to walk. I kept looking back to the clubhouse and suddenly noticed the car was gone. Then I heard a lot of commotion and voices and sirens near our house and ran back. Maybe they found Nancy, I thought. When I got to our house, sure enough, there was Nancy with nothing but her bathrobe on. Her underwear was gone.

"C'mon, and be quiet," the voice said. It sounded like it could be my mother's voice, but then, again, it was the middle of the night and I was in a deep sleep. I always slept like that – totally oblivious to the world. A bomb could drop and I'd never know it. But there it was again, that voice, and this time I realized I was moving with the voice and that I was walking sort of toward the kitchen. I was really in a dazed state, sleeping as soundly as I did. As I became fully awake, I realized I was going to the kitchen and now I feel the arm that is wrapped around my head from behind and a hand that is covering my mouth as we are heading out the back door by the kitchen. I screamed into his hand. "If you do that again, you're dead," said the voice as he held a knife to my head.

Realization comes slow when you are eleven years old; your mind says one thing and your senses another. At first I thought I was having a nightmare but then, I realized, *No, this is really happening, I'm being kidnapped from my home.* He began dragging me across the patio behind the master bedroom, my feet scrapping across the concrete floor. The stranger with me is in his twenties or early thirties with long blondish hair, beard, and mustache. Nothing too terribly uncommon about his looks. He has hold of my arm and says, "Come on! Come on!" (Later some of the neighbors who heard us walk by said they thought someone was walking their dog.) I knew he had a knife from our kitchen, and I was really scared yet almost unwilling to think about that. I was more concerned about where we were going and why.

We walked past a big wooden spool – a child's play toy – and climbed a fence and dropped down into the mud. They found our footprints there later. We walked for what seemed like quite a while and he kept muttering, "The drug dealers are after me."

I suddenly realized I was holding his T-shirt. I don't remember quite how I got it, but it had blood all over it. He was leading the way, and I remember a thought or voice within me shouting *Drop it. Drop it. Just do it! He won't see you,* so I did; I dropped it. He never noticed nor asked about it."

Finally we end at his destination. (Later I learned we had circled back and were basically in my back yard at an empty house kitty-corner to our backyard and right next to the cop's house. Kind of ironic isn't it?) He places me on the floor of a large room. I remember him removing my underwear (which I always slept in) thinking how terribly wrong this was and that what he was doing wasn't right. I was desperately trying to stop him when he asked me, "How old are you?"

I said, "Eleven."

"Eleven!" The number literally exploded from his mouth and he, to my utter disbelief, stopped what he was doing. He literally froze on the spot for a few seconds. Then he got up, grabbed me to my feet, and headed outside. He didn't pick up the knife but I didn't know this until later. We saw headlights and people in the direction of my house, and he made me crouch low behind hedges as we raced toward the clubhouse where he'd parked his car. I'll never forget that car. It was white, really old with tail fin sides and round headlights, kind of a low roof – elongated a bit. As we got in the car, my robe caught in the door. I panicked thinking I would somehow fall out. He started the car and asked me, "If I let you go will you promise not to tell anyone?"

I said I wouldn't.

"What will you tell your mother?"

I said I would tell her I was sleepwalking and got lost. He must have believed me because we didn't drive very far when he stopped the car and I got out.

I tried to figure out where I was when I saw some lights in the distance. All I could think about was getting home, yet at the same time panicked as to how I was going to explain to Mom where my underwear was. I finally found some familiar streets and followed them through to the shortcut, which led to the bushes by our house. I remember jumping through the bushes to find police everywhere and my mom incredibly upset.

My romantic full moon turned into a full-blown nightmare. There was mass confusion, police, sirens, an ambulance, Nancy crying hysterically, etc. and then there we were in the emergency room where they said Nancy needed to be checked for rape. They took her to a separate room. I wanted to go in with her but they wouldn't let me. I remember how I almost broke down the door when I heard my Nancy scream.

The Eleventh Hour!

I thought the hardest thing I went through that night was the attempted rape, but I'm not sure that was the case. You see the minute I returned, my life became a daily torture and what seemed hell on earth. First of all, I had to tell my mom about the things he did; things I didn't know how to describe. Then the trip to the emergency room; that was where I felt they finished what the rapist didn't accomplish. Then there were the cops trying to get me to say I had a fight with my mom and really just ran away. (They didn't believe me because about fifteen other girls were raped and then killed and some of their body parts were found in the desert. I found out later these girls were thirteen years and older.)

I don't remember but I guess they gave me something to help me sleep that night.

I was troubled most of the night wondering how Nancy would respond to all that had happened to her. So, the next morning I asked her, "Honey, I want to know how you feel about the man that did this to you."

She said, "Mom, this man is very, very sick. He kept saying 'The dope dealers are after me,' over and over again. I'm going to pray for him; he needs help, and if I pray for him, he might get caught, and if he gets caught, he'll get the help he needs and he won't hurt anyone ever again." I don't recall the exact words I said to her after that statement except to tell her that her faith in God was stronger than I'd ever expected, and that He would honor that faith. I thought to myself, Nancy will be all right.

The next day they found the bloody shirt, the footprints of where we were and eventually, the kitchen knife. I guess when they found all the evidence they finally believed me. Yet, they still made me take a lie detector test and had drawing artists come to my grade school to sketch the guy. After that I had to view a line-up of men where each guy was instructed to say, "Come on. Come on."

Then I was taken to Tucson, Arizona where I went through the same thing. There was one guy who looked so much like the one that took me I almost said, "He's the one," but then I really wasn't sure and didn't want to convict an innocent man. As it turned out, the one who looked so much like him was a detective or someone connected with the police department. I just wanted it all to end. The police did have me (unknown to my parents) talk to a girl named Nancy, (coincidence) who said the same thing happened to her. But I think this was a set-up by the police to see if I would tell her the same story. I never talked to her again but did find out that this guy had killed all the other girls. I was the only eleven-year-old. The others were all teenagers. They said that my age was what spared me. If he had taken my sister Mary, she would have been raped and killed; she was thirteen, but she looked like she was ten. She slept closest to the door, but he had deliberately gone to my bed across the room from hers because I looked older.

My dad was sent home from Vietnam for a couple of weeks because of this, but all I understood was

The Eleventh Hour!

that my parents hadn't a clue what to do with this situation. So basically, I thought they did nothing. Mom did tell me years later that they had the police watching our house day and night for six months; that he did come back once but he escaped their grasp and they never saw him again. She said she had also alerted the church counselors to keep an eye out for me.

Dad returned to Vietnam and when he came back in July of 1972, we moved to Nebraska where I completed school with minimal problems. Mom kept me on a pretty tight leash. The only place I really found some freedom was going with my sister Mary to her Agape Players group. This was an evangelistic singing, drama, outreach group that traveled to different areas. I loved the songs and the feeling of doing something good for others, but that too, eventually ended. As I got older, I resented not being allowed out past ten (and I was in the twelfth grade). I could only watch G-rated movies and lived a basically sheltered or grounded existence; Mom's way of protecting me I guess, but (and she agrees with me today) a big mistake.

When I finally graduated and turned eighteen, I moved into my own apartment. I was a girl/woman with some major problems hidden beneath the surface, but I didn't know it. I didn't realize how many hang-ups I had about guys and sex. I'd stuffed them inside of me for so long, they were ready to erupt, and my dad, who had a problem with alcohol, didn't help the situation any. I wanted someone to pay for messing up my life and decided that someone was going to be a man.

I purposely started down a path as far away from God as I could get. It was hard to believe that I had Christ in my heart all these times. I had accepted him at age ten but shelved Him not too long after the rape incident, figuring He just wasn't available. I deliberately went with the wrong crowd with one goal in mind. I wanted revenge. I was determined to take any guy and every guy and make them suffer the way I had suffered. I specifically went for the bad ones, the ones who swore, had lots of control, and seemed just basically evil. I figured the worse they were, the sweeter the victory. But I never won. All through my twenties and thirties I found myself in situations where I was controlled by men, mostly in my jobs. They were so perverse something in my soul would scream *Get away! Run! Find a new job,* but at the same time, I would hear, *You can conquer this one and make him pay. This one will pay for the pain you were caused when you were little.* My mind was so gone that the last time I tried to conquer just about cost me my life, my marriage, and my family. I had no control and it was obvious that I never would have because each time the men were more powerful; more forceful. I was playing with fire.

The turning point came when my own daughter turned eleven. I fell apart. The past came crashing back into the present and I thought how I'd die if the same thing happened to her. It was truly the eleventh hour; something had to happen. God had my attention, finally. I was at Oak Hills Church in the middle of a fully packed anointing with oil service in the youth auditorium. My heart ached and pounded. Oh, I wanted to go forward and be anointed with oil so badly. I just wanted to change and not repeat this pattern anymore. I wanted desperately to feel the love of the Lord once again, but I couldn't get out of the chair. Why would He want me after I turned my back on Him, why should He love me when I ran away, not trusting Him? I remember someone sitting next to me – a woman who, sensing my battle offered to go up with me – I still couldn't move. I'm not sure how it happened but I did get up to the front and met with Pastor Kent who remembered me from a visit we made to Oak Hills years ago. He directed me to a counselor.

The counselor listened tenderly and patiently as I shared what I had done, the relationships I tried to control, how it had caused me grief and unbearable pain that I had come to rely on as normal, and how I was playing two parts, living two lives; the life I let others see and the life no one knew about (except the Lord). I asked the counselor to be there for my husband Richard because I had to tell him about all the stuff I had done in trying to change what had happened to me in my childhood. Richard never knew about all the men that were abusing me at various jobs; he had no idea. I had hid it from him and others. I lived a lie for years. The Bible says, "There is a way that seems right to a man, but in the end it leads to death" (Prov.14:12). I felt I was on my way to that death.

On the advice of my counselor I finally wrote Rich a letter, telling him about all the awful things I'd done, telling him I was sorry – wishing he wouldn't cast me aside knowing I deserved nothing less. How could he love me –the disgrace of a life I had led? I just knew he would leave me. He was always so kind and good, never deserving a wife who was so very messed up. My counselor said I was a "city without walls" – vulnerable to anything.

I remember having not only my counselor but our small group leader on standby to help Rich sort out everything I had shared in the letter. I went into our bedroom and sat on the floor crying as he read it, believing that after he read my confession of a life he knew nothing about, that it was over.

The door to our room opened slowly. *This is it,* I thought, *my eleventh hour.*

My husband gently picked me up off the floor, held me in his arms, and said, "Do you think I could ever leave you? I love you and I could never leave you."

None of the awful things I'd done mattered to him. It was as if they had never happened. Then he held me and we cried together, and I knew freedom like never before. Rich knew my worst, my darkest nights and yet, he still loved me and forgave me. I now understood. That's how Jesus loved me from the beginning. He too, knew my worst, my darkest nights, and yet He still loved me and forgave me. He knew what happened to me and why I walked away from Him. But He wanted to show me that He

The Eleventh Hour!

too, would never, ever, leave me nor forsake me, nor anyone else who comes to Him. He was with me that horrible night when I was just eleven, and it was in the eleventh hour that the demon in that man froze on the spot, and my life was spared.

It was hard for me to accept the fact that Jesus still loved me. I believe that's why he used my husband Rich to show Himself to me in a way I could understand. I truly saw Jesus' love through my husband's eyes and heart that night.

How about you? Have you given your heart to the Lord and then turned your back on Him. Or, maybe you've never even opened the door to let Him in. Will you wait until the eleventh hour and endure the pain, suffering, and torment that Nancy did, or will you surrender now and open the door of your heart to Him. He will never leave you nor forsake you. If you want to invite Him into your heart, just pray the following prayer: Dear Jesus, I open the door of my life to you. Please come in, forgive my sins and take control of my life. I receive you as my Savior and Lord and ask you to fill me with your Holy Spirit and accept me as your child.

Chapter Twelve

Ride'm Cowboy

Doug Moses

With his arms waving furiously and tears streaming down his face, Doug kept mouthing the words 'I can't walk. I can't walk.'"

Doug Moses went to sleep in the cab of his truck with a young lady sitting beside him. He woke up in a hospital bed with his mother standing next to him. She told him he'd been in a coma for seven days.

"What happened? How did I get here?" Little by little, with Mom's help, he was able to put the pieces together. The realization that he could have and probably should have died hung heavy on his heart.

What if I had died? The thought of who would have been standing next to me when I woke up in – is too scary to think about. Why? My life consisted of drugs and alcohol. I was labeled wild child, party animal. I had no specific interest in anything except horses, and I was drawn to them almost as much as I was to drugs and alcohol. I had an intense desire to work with these beautiful animals, but when I tried to mix the two, it didn't work. It had to be either horses or parties. So what did I choose? The wild animal part.

For years I was like a wild and crazy horse running on a senseless track with people I thought were friends. I raced along with no direction, no purpose, no destination, no victories, and no losses: just an aimless journey day after day.

My adventures ended in January 1989 when this young lady and I drove up into the mountains near Flagstaff, Arizona. It was late when we decided to return. As we started down the mountain, it began to snow. Since I was already tired, I thought it would be a good idea to pull over and rest for a while. I spotted a cafe nearby and parked. As I slid over into the center of the cab of my truck, I asked her to wake me after a couple of hours or when it stopped snowing. She didn't want to wait. It was close to 2:00 A.M. and after I fell sound asleep she (in a fit of impatience) crawled over me into the driver's seat and began driving through the storm. The storm got worse and within a very short time, she lost control. In that moment, she either jumped or fell out of the truck as it careened off a cliff and down a steep embankment rolling over and over and over again.

The police officer said that as the truck descended, the transmission broke through the firewall and pinned me in the corner of the floor. It crushed my ankle as it proceeded to roll at an incredible rate of speed to the base of the canyon, approximately 164 feet. The officer said if I hadn't been pinned to the floor that I would have been killed. The truck was totaled but I was somewhat protected in that corner. Nevertheless, I was seriously injured. The odds of anyone finding me were not in my favor. I was unconscious and trapped in the middle of a snowstorm at the bottom of a canyon. The snow would quickly cover the tracks where I'd gone over the cliff. It was close to 3:00 A.M. How many people would be traveling down a mountain at that hour in that kind of weather, and even if they were, how many would notice? The tracks would be long gone by morning.

Do you believe in miracles? Angels? I do. I hadn't been down there very long when, of all things, an ambulance came by. What an ambulance was doing coming down that snowy mountain at three o'clock in the morning is a question only God can answer. Miraculously, the driver saw my tire tracks. Though visibility was poor, he and his assistant decided to investigate. They looked over the edge and saw my crumpled truck. Somehow they made it down the steep hillside, looked into the truck, and saw my battered body squashed in the floorboard. I don't know who these men were. I don't know how they got me out, and I don't know what happened to them or the young lady I was with. But, I believe that ambulance was sent by God.

While in the hospital, I learned that my roommate had moved out and taken all of my personal belongings with him. Everything I owned was gone except for the fact that I was alive. My wonderful mom, who I'd given nothing but grief in the past, bought me three pairs of sweat outfits, and except for her constant visits, nobody called or came to see me. All my "friends" were gone. Nobody could be found. I felt alone and destitute. After three months in a wheel chair (in March of 1989) I was flown by MediVac Aircraft to Mercy San Juan Hospital in Sacramento, California where, after a short time, I was released.

A wheelchair can be very confining to the body but mentally Doug was still racing. Like a horse on a merry-go-round, haunting mirrors reflected the shadows of his life, endless circles of emptiness. As he searched for answers, he happened to think of a former friend.

I could still picture his smile as he told me he had quit drugs and alcohol and was now a Christian. Somehow he'd started life over again and seemed to be at peace with himself. I decided to try to contact him. When he returned my call, he said he'd come to see me and he did, even while I was still in the wheelchair. He offered to share how he started over again if I were willing to go to church with him. Being really curious and eager to know what happened, I agreed, and one Sunday he and his wife picked me up for church. After the service, as I sat in my wheelchair, I began to cry. The minister was inviting people to come and kneel at the altar and accept the Lord. With my arms waving furiously and tears streaming down my face, I kept mouthing the words, "I can't walk. I can't walk." I kept on crying and begging the Lord to let me live and walk again. Then, all of a sudden, someone came down to pray with me, and slowly and earnestly I said, "Lord, Jesus, I'm a loser. I almost died. Tell me why I'm here. Show me why you let me live. I can't make it without you. Forgive me for wasting my life that you gave me. I need a father in my life, and I can't do it on my own anymore. I don't want to die. If you are for real, you will help me to help myself," and I pleaded and begged for forgiveness.

Over the next three years I had three reconstructive surgeries to rebuild my legs. During this time I wanted a Bible more than anything else and kept calling friends that I knew were Christians. I wanted to be around them and continued to look for others that I could fellowship with, and the Lord blessed me. My mother, who supported me through all of this, renewed her relationship with Jesus. We began to pray together and developed a new and stronger bond as mother and son. I remember her telling me, "This is the only thing that has ever worked for you in your whole life. I've renewed my faith and my walk with the Lord because of watching you over the past three years. In all your life, I've never seen you strive for anything harder than in the way you've sought the Lord."

I discovered many wonderful Christian organizations. Never had I been so loved, accepted nor seen such a willingness to help. But, I still wanted to know the reason my life was spared. I knew God had something in mind. It wasn't long before He began to bring people, places, and events across my path to show me what it was. He was getting ready to put this horse on a new track under the direction of a new Master. Little did I know then, His plan would lead to the very desire of my heart and a wonderful way to serve the Lord. While I could still barely walk, a young man by the name of Brian Peterson invited me to CRA that summer. CRA is a Christian running camp known today as CTM or Christian Team Ministries. Brian introduced me to Chris Vogt, the director of CRA and to a young man named Todd Noonan, both of whom were also members of CBMC (Christian Businessmen's Committee). When Brian told Nick about me, Nick said "If there's a guy that can barely walk that just came out of a wheelchair and is on fire for the Lord, I'd like to meet him." Well I did meet him, and Nick gave me a feeling of being needed and wanted and assigned me the firewood responsibilities. Through his love and willingness to accept me in my poor physical condition, (not knowing if I would ever have full use of my legs again), he is one of the many reasons I stayed with the Lord. And so is Todd. Their friendship and prayerful support were incredible. I had never experienced such consistency in a friend and eagerly pursued CRA and where the Lord wanted me to be.

But I got sidetracked when I met a young lady I thought was designed just for me. So I moved out of the area, ran from under the covering of Christ, and tried once again to make it on my own. "There is a way that seems right to a man, but in the end it leads to death" (Prov. 14:120). This new "filly" had me racing down the wrong track once again. I took such a beating mentally, spiritually, and financially, the only thing I knew to do was to go back to where I first met the Lord and the people who had so lovingly supported me. To my surprise, they received me with open arms, no questions asked. Through earnest prayer, I sought a career driving eighteen-wheelers. CBMC and CRA continued to accept me, love me and pray with me and then unexpected doors began to open.

One Sunday I happened to see a newsletter lying on a table in church. I couldn't ignore the title, *Cowboys for Christ*. Cowboys always had horses. I wanted to know more about this organization. As I picked up the article, a lady by the name of Jody Gimmer came by. She'd just had surgery on her leg and needed help moving a horse she purchased. I volunteered, and to my surprise, she let me assist her in catching and loading the horse. Shortly after that, I met a Christian farrier (horseshoer) at CBMC. He was willing to teach me all I needed to know about handling horses. He said he was also very familiar with Cowboys for Christ. He taught me how to establish a foundation and an outreach for Cowboys for Christ in Northern California.

That was only the beginning. He then assisted me in knowing about professional rodeos, covered wagon ministries, cattle drives, and all aspects of equestrian competition. Farmers and forest rangers, I discovered, were also involved with Cowboys for Christ. They held Sunday morning services at many rodeo events, including those held at high schools and various fairgrounds. They assisted neighbors and friends with cattle drives and were involved in 4H and FFA clubs throughout many locations. In addition, they gave Sunday morning presentations at equestrian exhibitions all over the United States.

Project RIDE is one of their specialties and one of my favorite areas of the ministry. It is specially designed for handicapped children. RIDE has proven to be very beneficial therapy for children with extreme disabilities and handicaps. After someone has volunteered their personal horse and their services at no charge, a registered nurse and volunteer or two will bring a wheelchair stricken child to an arena and mount that child in the saddle. They will then walk with that horse and child and work with them over a period of hours. It's been proven that this type of therapy has actually increased the child's physical capabilities.

I finally had my answer, and whether a "Cowboy for Christ," working with handicapped kids, or driving an eighteen-wheeler, I want to continue to live in Christ's corral and race on the only track that will end in eternal life with Him. I want to serve Him by helping others run in the right direction.

How about you? Are you on that wide fast track going nowhere? There's definitely a wide track out there, and countless runners are falling by the wayside. "Enter through the narrow gate. For wide the gate...that leads to destruction, and many enter through it. But...narrow the road that leads to life, and only a few find it" (Matt. 7:13, 14). You can continue on a worthless course and an endless journey with no destination, no hope, and no future now or later. Or, you could enter Christ's stables and let Him show you how to win the race for life. "God has given us eternal life and this life is in His Son. He who has the Son has life; he who does not have the Son of God does not have life" (1 John 5:11, 12). If you would like to enter Christ's corral and let Him be in charge of your life, just earnestly pray the following prayer and He will make himself known to you: Dear Jesus, I open the door of my heart to you. Please come in, forgive my sins, and take control of my life. I receive You as my Savior and Lord and ask You to fill me with your Holy Spirit and accept me as your child.

Chapter Thirteen

From Chicken Bones to Ironman

"And I chose the Ironman Triathlon World Championship in Hawaii."

Ken Campbell, oldest of four children, was raised in Sacramento. He attended Mira Loma High and then obtained his Bachelor of Science degree in biochemistry from the University of California, Davis in 1979. Four years later, in the spring of 1983, he expected to graduate with a dental degree from Northwestern University of Illinois, but a red light and two trucks suddenly changed his plans.

※

We were going to be the best father/son team in Sacramento and, in addition to my dental work with

Dad, I believed I was going to go into mission work in Central America. I had my life so well planned—so sure of everything that I told God, "Lord, I know this is what you want me to do." But it wasn't what He wanted; it was what I wanted.

About one and one-half months before my graduation from Northwestern, I was coming home late from a basketball game. I was asleep in the back seat of a Ford Mustang driven by my good friend, Joedy Stegman. Her brother, Tom, was next to her in the front seat. We stopped for a red light. Next to us was a gasoline truck. Without warning, another truck, a big flat bed, came at freeway speed and rammed right into the back of that tanker. About eight thousand gallons of gas exploded sending flames one hundred feet into the air. The impact blew out house and car windows all around, including ours. Gasoline and flames engulfed the car. Joedy, who got out on the truck side, was closest to the flames. She shouted, "Ken, you've got to get out of there." I don't know how I got out of that two-door vehicle from the back seat but somehow, by the grace of God, I did and ran and rolled on the ground. It seemed like forever waiting for the ambulance. While rolling in the snow, Joedy said start praying and we began to pray out loud right there. I remember saying, "Lord, take me now, it hurts too bad; I know I'm going to go anyway."

In the emergency room, the doctor said Joedy was burned over 90 percent of her body and I was burned over 70 percent. Her twenty-one-year-old brother, Thomas, suffered minor burns. I knew from my training that anyone burned over 70 percent rarely made it. Have you ever burned your finger or part of your body while cooking or doing some kind of project? Remember how painful that was? Imagine that over 70 percent of your body. The pain was indescribable and incredibly unbearable. I believed I wasn't going to live and called the nurse over and said, "Listen, I'd like you to tell my father, mother, brother and sister, and my friends that I love them and will miss them. I know I haven't a chance of making it and this hurts. I'm just going to get out of here now."

You know how nurses are; she said, "Oh, you're going to be fine."

And somewhat sarcastically I said "Yeah, sure, right!" And then I said, "I'm going to check out now and turned my head and started praying, "Dear Lord, I'm willing to go so just take me now and get me out of this pain." Obviously, the Lord didn't answer the way I expected and waking up in a burn unit the next day was quite a shock.

First of all, when you get burned, your body gets edematous; that means swollen. My head was the size of a basketball; my arms, legs, my whole body was swollen beyond recognition. There was a feeding tube in my nose, a trach tube in my throat (so I could breathe), IVs in my chest, chest tubes in my chest (because my lungs had collapsed), a catheter, arterial lines in my toe, and monitors all over me, along with a bunch of others. When the doctors said, "It's time for your prognosis,"

I said, "OK, what's the prognosis?"

"Well," they said, "First of all, you're probably not going to make it."

Again, somewhat sarcastically, I said, "Great! I already knew that."

"And, if you do make it, you're probably not going to practice dentistry."

My mother confirmed that prediction when she said my fingers looked, "like chicken bones that were held over the fire too long."

I couldn't believe it. I'd gone through four years of undergraduate school and four years of dental school and now I was being told I couldn't do what I'd been trained to do.

The second thing they said was, "Ken, we know you like running, biking, swimming and all sorts of other great outdoor sports.—Ken, be happy if you're walking." (I had been running ten miles a day and swimming fifty to one hundred laps, three times a week before the accident.)

I said, "I can't believe it, I'm not going to be able to do all those things I love."

And as if this wasn't enough, they said, "For two years you'll have to wear garments on your hands, face, and over your whole body. And, when those come off, you're going to have lots of scars."

I said, "There goes vanity, my dreams, goals, and aspirations." Then I said, "Now, what?"

Well, he started changing my dressings and said they'd have to do that every eight hours. This hurt a great deal so they gave me morphine and Valium to dull the pain. Then, once a week for about twelve to fifteen weeks, I'd go to surgery for skin grafts; they were extremely painful too.

When I thought I'd reached the bottom of the pit, I got the news that Joedy went to be with the Lord on April 27, just twenty-eight days after the accident. My mind couldn't handle that and I lost control. All I could think of was, *Hey, God, are you there? Do you even care? Are you trying to punish me for something, or are you just having fun with me or are you even in control?*

But God was in control because about that time someone gave me a poem called "Footprints." It's my favorite. It's about a man who dies and goes to heaven and then looks back on his life and sees two sets of footprints in the sand. He notices that during the roughest and toughest times of his life there was only one set of prints and he says, "Hey God, why when I had the roughest and toughest times in my life were there only one set of prints? I can't understand why, when I needed you most, that you would leave me."

And the Lord said, "Listen, my precious, precious child, it was during those times when things were so tough and rough that I was carrying you."

I believe that's what He was doing. He was in control and He was holding me in His arms as I lay in that deep dark pit, and to make me aware of His presence, He sent two pastors who came every day to read to me from the Bible. Mom and Dad would do the same. They'd come each day and read scriptures to me. At first, I didn't want to hear them. I rejected them because I felt that if God really cared for me, He wouldn't have me here. But, as they continued to open those precious words each day, they sank deep into my heart and began working in there. I believe my recovery began when I started saying, "Yes, God, You are there. You are in control." And they kept coming and reading those words, and I started believing them. Some of the verses became very special to me, such as Hebrews 4:16 that says, "So that we may receive mercy and find grace to help in time of need." And it did help as I struggled day by day during physical therapy.

After three months, my therapist said, "Ken, you're going to be leaving in about a month, what would you like to do?"

Since we'd become really good friends, I jokingly said, "Well, I'd like to run a six-minute mile. After all, I ran a marathon; in fact, twenty-six of them. So why can't I run just one?"

Almost with a laugh, she said, "Hey, know what? If I were you I'd be happy if I were just able to walk."

If you'd seen me, you would have agreed. I weighed about one hundred thirty pounds, my body was atrophied from lying in bed so long, and my muscles were very weak. If they just sat me up in bed it hurt. My upper body would crush my lower body, and I wouldn't be able to breathe. So I said, "What I'd like to do is to be able to get my diploma when they bring the graduation ceremony here to the hospital."

"We'll work on that," she said.

And work we did! She began working on my muscles. I'd have her come two or three times a day and on Saturdays and Sundays. My muscles began getting stronger and pretty soon she had me sitting up in bed, then sitting on the side, then taking a step, two steps, and then getting into a wheelchair which I needed to get to the room where my graduation would be held. She'd pull me up out of the chair and have me try to take the few steps I needed to get my diploma. I practiced over and over but wasn't happy about having to be pulled up out of my chair. She said, "Listen, if you can walk up to the podium to get your diploma, that's good enough."

"No," I said, "That's not good enough! I want to be able to stand up by myself." So, she put pillows under me and we practiced some more.

On the day of graduation I was able to rock back and forth in my chair until I could stand up and then walk those few steps to get my diploma. It may only have been five steps, but just being able to walk like that again was great. There had been so many things I took for granted—running, swimming, touch, sight, feel, etc. As I walked up to get my diploma, I thought about Joedy. I remembered how, just a few hours before the accident we were playing around in the snow and just having a great time putting it down each others back and rolling around in it, and then, all of a sudden, she was gone. So many things, so many people I took for granted. *God, please don't let me do that ever again.*

After four months, I was on my way back to California. As Mom sat next to me on the plane, I prayed, "Dear Lord, I can't believe I'd go through four years of dental school and not be able to practice; I can't believe You'd have me love outdoors so much and now can't do all those things." I said, "Lord, I want to walk again, to be able to run and to practice dentistry."

When I got home, I started setting little goals. I started sitting up on the bed, then walking up the street and back down, and I'd fall back in bed exhausted and that would be my workout for the day. Pretty soon I was walking up and down a couple of times, then around the block three to four times. Then I began working with a physical therapist again and when I was able to walk five miles, he said, "Ken, I think it's time you started running."

"Oh, no!" I said, "Every time I've tried to run I'd fall."

But this therapist, a big guy, about 6'5", wouldn't take no for an answer. He took a belt and strapped it around my waist and he'd have me run a few steps. I'd trip and fall and he'd pick up all one hundred thirty pounds of me and put me back down. And, I'd run again and trip and fall, and he'd yank me back up and put me down. Time and again, I'd trip and fall and he'd pick me up. Well, after about a week or so of this, I was running around the field and I'd trip just a few times. Pretty soon I was running so well he said, "You know what, you're going to have to find another running partner."

"Oh, great! Now what do I do?" But I got a good friend to start running with me and nineteen months after the accident (totally against the advice of a lot of doctors who said, "I read your chart and know what happened to you. It's impossible for you to do this. Don't do it."), I went back to Chicago and ran the Chicago Marathon – 26.2 miles.

Crossing that finish line made me realize that if God wants you to do something, He'll equip you for it. I was so thrilled, I couldn't stop thanking Him. The bottom line is, it doesn't matter who says you can't, if God wants it done (no matter how impossible), it's done! As I thought about the awesome strength and power he had given me during the race, I felt like He was saying, *Ken, you haven't seen anything yet. I want you to choose something that's totally impossible.* And I chose the Ironman Triathlon World Championship in Hawaii. This is a 2.4-mile swim in the ocean where sometimes its so rough people get seasick. After your swim, you get out of the water and onto your bike and you bike for 112 miles up this long hill and then back down. Some times the wind is so strong it will blow you off your bike and then, if that's not enough, you get on your running shoes and start running. You run 26.2 miles sometimes during incredible heat (It was 125 degrees when I ran October 10, 1987) and then, when you cross the finish line, you get a great big pat on the back and they say, "You're an Ironman!"

When I crossed that finish line, it was more than that for me. I felt like God's Ironman. I knew it was His iron (His words) that equipped me. He had given me an inner strength, a will, and supernatural power that far surpassed any kind of man-made iron or ability. Many people, not just doctors, tried to talk me out of the triathlon saying things like, "You can't handle the sun; the heat is too intense." (As a result of the burns, my sweat glands didn't function anymore.) But, in spite of all the opposition, I felt God saying, *I want you to do this even though it seems impossible. We're going to do it!* And we did.

After that, I knew I couldn't stop there. There was another impossible race I had to finish – father/son dental team. Once again, I started to set goals and to work this time with an occupational therapist. "Faith without deeds is useless" (James 2:20). He had me take little tweezers with which I took little pins from a little jar and transferred them into another jar, and that's how my manual dexterity developed.

But, let's go back a few steps. Remember how my mom said my fingers looked like chicken bones that were held over the fire too long? Well, the doctors wanted to amputate my hands but my friends came and would pray twenty-four hours outside my room and even started singing songs. Messages came back to me about their prayers: "Lord, it's impossible that he's not going to have his hands to be able to practice dentistry. We believe you want him to."

And they kept on praying until the doctor came back and said, "OK, it looks like we won't have to amputate his hands." They were so excited, but then he said, "But he is going to lose a few fingers on his right hand."

Again, my friends said, "That's impossible, he needs those fingers to practice," and they kept right on praying.

Miraculously, the doctor came back a third time and said, "Well, he's not going to lose his fingers, but even so, we believe he's not going to be able to practice dentistry because he'll have very limited dexterity."

They kept on praying and believing even though they knew they'd have to wait quite a while for that answer. I love people who pray like that because God answers that kind of praying. "Without faith, it is impossible to please God" (Heb. 11:6). And so, by faith, I began working with this occupational therapist and his tiny pins and tweezers. Little by little my dexterity returned and I began working with some of my dental instruments.

When I was doing pretty well my therapist said, "It's time for you to go back to dental school."

As usual, no one believed I could do it but I was accepted for a year's internship and started working with plastic teeth. It wasn't long before they said, "Hey, maybe you should start working on real teeth."

"Great!" I said, and I began working on real people.

That was scary at first but after a year they said, "Your work is as good as, if not better than a lot of senior dental students."

I said, "Wow! I can't believe it." It was hard going back and relearning all that stuff again but, after hearing those words, "Ken, you're ready," I went racing back to California where I began practicing dentistry with my father, Dan Campbell, thereby completing still another impossible goal.

And, believe it or not, I was even able to go and do some mission work in Central America. (I know I'm going to go back there again some time.) Of all my original plans, the only ones that didn't materialize were the ones Joedy and I had made. God had something else in mind as He waited for me to give him 100 percent of my trust. From the time He took Joedy home, He was preparing a special partner for me to spend the rest of my life with, a special someone who would look beyond my scars and see His beauty and His iron in my life. He brought Joedy and me together for a purpose, and that purpose was fulfilled a short time before her death.

We met about one and one-half years before the accident. I'd invite her to our Christian

Medical Society and to Bible study but she never seemed interested. As we became better friends, we went out to dinner one night and when we sat down, the first thing I said to her was "Joedy, are you a Christian?"

"Oh, sure, I'm a Christian, I go to church."

"Oh, great," I said, "you go to church, but that's not the answer to my question. Are you a Christian?"

Again, she said, "Sure, I go to church and do good things."

I said, "Joedy, you know what? Going to church doesn't make you a Christian any more than going to MacDonald's makes you a hamburger."

"OK," she said, "What is a Christian?"

"Being a Christian is having Jesus Christ in your heart and having that personal relationship with Him."

Joedy said, "Hey, I've gone to church all my life and haven't heard about this Jesus, but just this past week His name has been coming up and I'd like to know about all this." She was so excited; we talked about Jesus for the rest of the evening. I told her what the Lord meant to me and about the relationship she could have. "This is neat," she said. "Is there something I could read about this?" I gave her a book about faith. She read it that night and then asked if there was another book she could read.

After reading that, I introduced her to my friend Joan, who began reading Bible verses in the book of John with her. I was really hopeful of her finding that relationship with the Lord when she said she had to leave for her internship in physical therapy. I panicked, but wherever she went, there was always a Christian nearby taking care of her. God is really faithful and one day Joedy went to a church where the pastor gave an altar call after a very Christ-centered message. Joedy, prompted by the Holy Spirit, walked down the aisle and committed her life to the Lord. When she called to tell me about it, I walked around for weeks singing "Amazing Grace."

And it was amazing because it was the first time in my life I'd opened my mouth and told someone about the Lord. I'm so glad I did because we used to joke about living to the ripe old age of ninety or one hundred. Neither of us anticipated anything that would change our lives so soon after she made that decision. The Bible tells us that our lives are but a vapor, which appears for a while and then vanishes away. I believe God's purpose in bringing Joedy into my life was so that she could know Him and to make me realize through all of this the importance of not only having my life straight before the Lord but also the importance of telling others. I know that if anything happened to me and it's my last breath that I'm going to be in heaven. Others need to know that, and I'm so thankful I told Joedy about Jesus because the Bible says that when we get to heaven we'll have bodies and we'll be able to recognize each other. One of the first things I'm going to do is to find Joedy and tell her how good it is to see her and how thankful I am that I opened my mouth and told her about Jesus. There are so many people around us, friends and family; they need to hear this message and maybe you are reading this and you don't know the Lord, but you can know Him. He said He would reveal Himself to those who earnestly seek Him. Your personal relationship can start with the following prayer: Dear Jesus, I open the door of my heart to you. Please come in, forgive my sins, and take control of my life. I receive You as my Savior and Lord and ask You to fill me with your Holy Spirit and accept me as Your child.

Has this story made an impact on your life? Have you made your plans and set your goals for the future? Do they include the Lord? Most people prepare a will stating what's to be done with their possessions when they die. But what about the "will" inside of you? Does it include arrangements for your eternal body and where it will be? Will your bones rejoice in new surroundings in heaven one day, or will they be agonizing in hell like chicken bones that were held over the fire too long? The flames that enveloped Joedy and Ken lasted only a short while, and though the ongoing pain and damage they caused seemed endless at the time, they were temporary. The flames and pain that await those who die without Christ are eternal. You have a choice while you are still alive. "For it is with your heart that you believe and are justified, and it is with your mouth that you confess and are saved" (Rom. 10:10). "It is appointed for men to die once and after this comes judgment" (Heb. 9:27 NASB). Jesus said, "I stand at the door and knock. If anyone hears my voice and opens the door, I will come in" (Rev. 3:20). You can't afford to wait until tomorrow; you may not be here!

When Ken allowed the Lord to be the controlling force, to be the iron in his life, and dependent on His strength rather than his own ideas, the Lord not only gave him back his original goals and desires but increased them over and beyond what he could have imagined. That "someone the Lord had been preparing" was brought to his side not long after he ran the triathlon. Sandy Duncan (and as of June 22, 1991, Mrs. Ken Campbell) looks like someone you might find on the cover of a magazine. But more evident than her outer beauty is the love she has for the Lord. She was attracted to Ken because of his strong commitment to God and His goals. When they met at Friday Night Singles, a Christian ministry the Lord called Ken to about three years ago, Sandy had just completed a ten-year goal of her own which was to own and operate a horse ranch. She was drawn to Ken's determination and discipline since this was very much a pattern in her own life. From the moment they met, Sandy says she never noticed the scars because they disappeared beneath his other qualities that she admired and respected and which were so outstanding.

God blessed their relationship and Ken realized the fulfillment of another impossible dream as he and Sandy exchanged marriage vows and she became Mrs. Ken Campbell, the woman God prepared just for him.

Chapter Fourteen

Big Jim Oren and the Little Green Submarine

*Wh*enever it rained during winter, the basement of our house in North Hollywood, California, flooded. My step dad (I was two when my father died) built a flume to help pump the water out. This made a great place to float my little green submarine, and I was busy doing that one Saturday afternoon when the pastor of the church my step dad took us to came by for a visit.

This very legalistic church always talked about the wrath of God but never the love of Jesus. When the pastor saw me floating my submarine, he came up from behind and said, "Jimmy, if you do this on the Sabbath Day, you're going to go to hell."

Well, I was only eight years old but decided then and there that, "I don't want any part of a God who would send me to hell for such a little thing." And from that day on my attitude toward God changed course, and things I saw and experienced in that church helped me to believe I'd made the right decision. Among other things, women couldn't wear dresses any higher than their ankles, sleeves had to be down to the wrist, make-up was not permitted, and cutting their hair short was out of the question. They looked like a bunch of old fuddy-duddies who never smiled. (And why should they, there was no joy in their lives.) Mom was the only one who was different. She loved Jesus and showed it in the way she treated me.

I can't remember a church service where someone wasn't rebuked and left crying. All I ever heard was constant bickering, and we couldn't go to the theater or use radios. My parents didn't see anything wrong with a radio and eventually hid one in their closet, which made them feel like hypocrites. We even had dietary restrictions; no pork or bacon, etc. I saw God as big bully with a baseball bat and didn't want any part of Him. But as I said, thanks to Mom, I saw Jesus differently. He represented love through Mom's love for me and so I didn't see Jesus and God as one and the same at that time in my life.

When I was twelve, I began sneaking out of my room at night and going to the movies, which, like the hidden radio, I saw nothing wrong with. At fourteen, my stepbrother (who was seven years older than me) had gotten married and was now divorced. He invited me to come to Idaho because he was lonely. I jumped at the chance to see what I thought real life was like. He provided money for me to go to the movies almost every afternoon, and since I could easily pass for eighteen (weighing some 175 lbs and able to shave), I also began experimenting with tobacco and whiskey, followed by my first sexual encounter with a sixteen-year-old girl. I was in the real world all right, and I lived for no one but me, Big Jim Oren.

By nineteen, I served in the Navy Air Force during the Korean War, got married and had two children, a boy in 1955 and a girl in 1957. The marriage ended in divorce and out of loneliness, I married again, only to have it end in divorce as well. I was unfaithful to both of my wives and knew it was wrong, but sin just gets easier the more you get into it. Though I wasn't the first to commit adultery, when I caught my first wife in bed with another man, I decided to do the same. That doesn't make it right, but my masculinity was threatened, and I felt I had to prove that I could still be attractive to other women. When my second wife moved in with her boyfriend, I lost all respect for women and just didn't care anymore.

My life was continuously on the ragged edge after that. Motorcycles, hot tubs, and speedboats occupied most of my time. I was known as a two-fisted drinker who burned the candle at both ends. When I got out of the service I became a heavy-duty trucker. Weekends were spent on various lakes and river areas involving water skiing, drag racing, and heavy boozing. I specifically remember one incident in 1955 in San Fernando. While riding with a motorcycle gang, one of the guys challenged me to a race. Neither of us wore helmets. I was wearing a T-shirt, a pair of sickle boots, and Levis. I won the race, but in the process of shutting down, we collided with each other, and I went off the bike at better than one hundred miles per hour on a two-lane highway. My motorcycle was traveling south in the southbound lane, and my body south in the northbound lane. I rolled head-over-heels for better than 100 yards. All I thought of was dying by hitting a car with my body. In fact, I should have been killed. Only by God's grace was there no traffic on that particular road at that time.

When I arrived at the hospital two hours later, I had a broken ankle, pulled ligaments in my right leg, and asphalt burns over 30 percent of my back, hands, arms and legs. But that didn't stop me.

I went on like this for the next fifteen years until I was forty-two. That's when I met Liz. A co-worker (who happened to be Liz's brother) introduced us, and seventeen days later I married her thinking, *If it works, fine; if it doesn't, that's OK, too I've already been through two divorces and one more won't make much difference.* But there was something different about Liz, and two months after the wedding, I decided I really wanted to make this marriage work. About the same time, however, Liz developed some female problems and needed a total hysterectomy, which completely changed her personality. As months went by, things became more and more difficult between us.

Approximately one and one-half years later, in January of 1976, Liz, her daughter from a former marriage, and I decided to take a vacation in Hawaii. Two days after our arrival in Maui, Liz was stricken with a physical ailment that threw us all for a loop. It was a type of chemical imbalance on the order of a nervous breakdown. Our vacation turned into a nightmare. We couldn't keep clothes on Liz. She just refused to wear clothing and cursed and screamed at everyone, including one of my best friends.

Realizing I'd come up against something so weird and foreign, something for the first time that Big Jim couldn't handle on his own, I found myself on my knees looking for the God I hadn't wanted anything to do with. I searched back into my past to my knowledge of Christ, the one my mom believed in so faithfully. I began to pray and asked Him to deliver Liz from this crazy sickness promising that if He did, I would make a deal with Him—I would serve Him to the best of my ability. I was tired of the life I was living anyway; smoking, drinking, and many other things. To my surprise, Liz did start getting better, but I procrastinated about serving Him for more than a year until Easter Sunday in 1977. That day I knew I had to go to church and told Liz, "I've got to go to church. I don't care where, but I've got to go."

During the service, while the pastor was explaining the suffering and pain Christ went through at Calvary, I experienced a vision and began to cry. I hadn't shed any tears in over twenty years, but I saw Jesus (the only one I ever associated with love during my younger years) hanging on the cross. I couldn't distinguish His nose from His eyes and His head was swollen to twice the size of normal as a result of the beatings and poison from the crown of thorns. The vision was so real it seemed I could reach out and touch His face, and in that moment I realized He had truly died for Big Jim Oren. Somehow, I also knew that if I received Him, my sins would be washed away forever because of the blood He shed for them. I cried uncontrollably because He was willing to take me just as I was, still heavily in bondage to tobacco and alcohol. People were looking at me but I didn't care, and although Liz was still not completely healed, I knew I wanted Jesus for myself. So, at approximately 10:20 A.M. that Easter Sunday morning, that's exactly what I did. I asked Him to come in, forgive my sins, and then promised to live my life for Him from that day on. I knew my sins were forgiven and within six months I was totally tobacco and alcohol free. I was so excited I wanted to share Jesus with my buddies at work but they didn't want to hear about Him. I became an outcast and, as a matter of fact, they nicknamed me The Preacher.

I began making it a practice to read the Bible before work each morning and to be in church every Sunday. One year later, Liz gave her life to the Lord and was totally healed. One year after that, her daughter (whom I raised since age thirteen) gave her life to Christ, and a year after that, Liz's youngest son also accepted Him. And then, Liz's brother (the one who introduced me to her) made his commitment also.

I couldn't stop talking about the Lord no matter where I was. I wanted to keep my promise to Him and so got involved in a part-time hospital ministry in Reno, Nevada in 1979. However, my inner craving to serve Him full-time wouldn't go away, and in 1987 while working in heavy construction dump-trucking and also doing excavation and paving at the Washoe County Jail facility in Reno, I decided to retire and just serve the Lord.

In 1988 we began attending a church in Truckee, California. We were very impressed with their many outreach ministries and fell in love with this body of believers. We wondered if there was a ministry here for us. Well, while Liz and I were traveling to Reno to do some shopping one day, we drove by the Washoe County Jail and I said, "Wouldn't it be neat if we could reach some of those inmates for Christ?" One Sunday morning a couple of weeks later, our church made a request for someone to help in the area of prison ministries. I had no doubt but what the Holy Spirit was speaking to me about this area and, when I saw that Liz agreed with me, I got involved. To my surprise, the ministry was at the very jail we talked about earlier and where I had previously worked, Washoe County Jail. And I'm still involved doing a weekly praise and worship service every Thursday night. I've seen many lives changed and many commitments to serve Jesus. Liz has since joined me in this ministry and we thank God from the bottom of our hearts.

What about you? Was there a little green submarine somewhere in your life that torpedoed your thoughts, plans, and dreams? When Jim's friends teased him about his faith in God by nicknaming him The Preacher, little did they realize that this was exactly what the Lord had in store for him. And, isn't it ironic that it was a preacher that initially destroyed his faith and love for God? Jim is now God's submarine and He created a flume for him to reach the submerged depths of men's hearts so they could know Christ, and pump out the garbage flooding their minds and hearts.

God has a plan for your life and will use anything and anyone to get you to realize how much He loves you and wants you to belong to Him, to make you realize He created you for good, not for evil; to be useful to yourself and to others; to be that special someone He created in His own image.

Did an enemy come along and destroy your dreams, your visions about the Lord, your talents and what you can do through Him? Take time to up periscope and set your sights above. It's time to surface into the Sonlight of His love and to know the freedom of acceptance and value in His sight. If you are not a Christian and want to know this kind of love then, in faith, pray the following prayer and start a new life in Him: Dear Jesus, I open the door of my heart to You. Please come in, forgive my sins, and take control of my life. I receive You as my Savior and Lord and ask You to fill me with Your Holy Spirit and accept me as Your child.

Chapter Fifteen

The Anchor Man

"He had huge, hideous, piercing green eyes and terrible teeth covered with moss."

Born June 26, 1931. Died August 8, 1982. Bob Whitten, former KRCA anchorperson, tells why this should have been his epitaph as he shares his walk through the Valley of the Shadow of Death.

Bob laughed as he ignored my outstretched hand and grabbed me in a big, warm bear hug. "Told you handshakes were no longer in my make up since I turned my life over to the Lord."

"Why did you do that?" I asked. "Your friend, Chuck Collings, says you never let anyone talk to you about God. What made you change your mind?"

Bob hesitated a moment and then said, "God got my attention while I was staying in a Sacramento motel with someone I had no business being with. I believe it was His way of putting an end to the many games I was playing. Chuck's right," he continued, "Until then, you couldn't mention God to me. Even though I was raised in a Christian home, church meant nothing to me; my parents went, so I went. Eventually I became an affirmed agnostic. I wasn't sure there was a God, but not sure there wasn't a God. Either way, it didn't matter. I didn't need anyone or anything, including a God I wasn't sure existed. In my senior year I'd planned on going to MIT. I drove east out of Dallas to KSST in Sulphur Springs and said, 'I want to work for you.' That started my radio career.

"A greeting from the U.S. Army sent me overseas. When I returned, I spent a year at KRLD in Dallas, after which I headed west, pulled into KCRA Channel 3 News, and was hired by Dave Hume as anchorperson. During my one and one-half years with them I ran for the Senate. Obviously, I didn't make it.

"After the Senate run, I went to work for Raleys and became their TV spokesman, writing and producing all their commercials. You know," he added, "I was quite a well-known TV and radio personality, with earnings in the six-figure bracket. I even had my own advertising business—Bob Whitten & Associates.

"I was respected and admired, always in the public eye, and though materially and socially strong, very weak of spirit, probably caused by a hidden inferiority complex. Sort of an extroverted introvert, you might say. Nothing satisfied me. I always had to have more and more to feed my quest for power. I gorged on praise, knowing the right people, making the right contacts, attending the right functions, etc. A wonderful wife, good marriage and family soon found no room in my itinerary, and it wasn't long before I found myself in that motel room where my game playing ended on August 8, 1982 when a very sudden unexpected stroke interrupted my socially prominent lifestyle and brought it to an abrupt finish. The stroke found its mark and scored a perfect bull's-eye, rendering me lifeless. I can only thank God that the person with me called an ambulance and got me to the hospital in time.

The next thing I remembered was the night I almost died. I was lying in bed in terrible pain and trying to sleep when I noticed a presence in the room. I opened my eyes to stare at a horrible figure standing beside my bed. He had huge, hideous, piercing green eyes and terrible teeth covered with moss. I pulled away as he reached out and said, 'I've come to take you away from all this pain.'

"Are you who I think you are?" I asked.

"Yes," he answered.

"I knew he was the one they called the Grim Reaper! Too frightened to move, I began to sob and cry, and for the first time I cried out to the God I had denied all my life. I prayed, 'God, help me please!'

"My cries brought the nurse who put me to sleep, and as I dozed off, I saw the figure go to the bed next to mine. The man in it was a big East Indian who also had a stroke and who kept pulling imaginary things off his arms, which he called jambees and baccoos. The next morning he was dead! I knew I had been spared, but he was gone! Did he go with the Grim Reaper? The thought propelled me out of bed and found me on my knees.

"Chuck's prayers for me were answered when, with tears streaming down my face, I asked Jesus to come into my life. I said 'Take my life, Lord; I turn it over to you.' And then, 'God, you've let me live this long, and I promise you right now that if you let me live, I'll spend the rest of my life serving you and benefiting others.' All my fears disappeared and I got better.

"The Twenty-third Psalm, 'Even though I walk through the valley of the shadow of death, I will fear no evil,' etc. had become my favorite. My game playing has been replaced with new extracurricular activities, such as visiting convalescent homes, attending Christian Businessmen's meetings, sharing my testimony, and daily thanking God for the wonderful wife He gave me. This beautiful woman had every reason to leave me, but instead forgave me and was faithful to stand by me and love me back to health. Now, when I open my eyes, the first thing I reach for is my Bible, and it's the last thing I read before going to bed at night. Most of all, I'm excited to be God's anchorman, sharing with others my walk through the Valley of the Shadow of Death in the hope that they, too, will weigh anchor in Christ."

In memory of Bob Whitten:

Bob Whitten is no longer with us. He passed through that valley mentioned in Psalm 23, just a few years after this story was given to me in July of 1986. I originally published it in a Christian newsletter called *The Encourager*. Bob never got to see the letter his sister, Betty Fink, wrote me in October of that year. I am reprinting it here in memory of Bob and in awe of the verse that says, "With God all things are possible" (Matt.19:26).

Dear Courier Editors:

A copy of your July Courier was mailed to me here in Texas, and I wanted you to know what a wonderful blessing it was to me. You see, your front-page article was about my brother, Bob Whitten. Your story was factual but the whole story is quite incredible and it is truly a giant Texas-size miracle that God got hold of this man!

I wept as I looked at his picture and read the story of his testimony to the changing power of Christ, and once again I thanked God for saving Bob out of darkness and into His glorious light!

I prayed for Bob for many, many years, but I must confess that sometimes I thought that it was absolutely hopeless; he was so closed to, and even scorned and sneered at any mention of God or Jesus. Finally I prayed, "God, do whatever You have to do," and that is when He allowed the stroke that brought Bob to the end of himself and in desperate need of the Lord.

Bob was truly an impossible case proving that all things are possible with God. Now that Bob is living his life for God, I never see an impossible case. My faith has really increased and my heart is so full to know that my brother will live forever with me and Jesus!

Thank you for your wonderful article, and may God continue to bless your paper, for surely it is an "Encourager."

Sincerely,
(Signed Betty Fink)
Betty J. Fink

CHAPTER SIXTEEN

FIRE AND ICE

Jim Mensie 1998, The Frozen "Chosen"

 $\mathcal{J}$ im Mensie was frozen twice, once by man, and once by the Lord. Join with me as we follow his incredible story of healing in the fire of God's love.

At the age of twelve I was already more than very girl conscious, and when this particular girl I was trying to impress invited me to go to church, I went. When I heard the Gospel, I responded and invited the Lord into my heart. But that was it! I didn't fully realize the impact of what I had done. I didn't yet really know the God I'd given my life to in that moment, and there was no one to help me to know Him, no influence of any kind. No one in my family knew God or anything about Jesus. So, I never read the Bible, never prayed, and eventually stopped going to church.

The sudden warmth of my one-time heart experience, a flame that should have been fanned by the bellows of the Bible, quickly disappeared. Like a coal taken out of the fire, it faded and grew cold, and by the age of fifteen, I'd successfully buried the Lord to where I no longer heard His voice (God gives us that choice!) even though He said He would never leave us nor forsake us. He never takes away our freedom to choose the path we want to follow.

Well, with Jesus tucked away in the darkest corner of my heart, girls became the light of my life, and as a junior in high school, drugs and drinking drowned any inhibitions I might have had. I loved doing drugs and drinking. I loved rock n' roll and girls and the whole shot. By age sixteen I had the privilege (or so I thought) of tasting the forbidden fruit of sex. We just reveled in all this darkness, not

Fire and Ice

knowing how it could suddenly and fatally snap our lifelines ending our existence.

By seventeen to eighteen years of age I'd OD'd (overdosed) on drugs a few times. On one particular occasion my lifeline almost did snap. I remember waking up stark naked in this bathtub full of ice. My friends, scared to death that I was going to die (and I was truly on my way out) and afraid to take me to a hospital for fear of the police, went to the liquor store and bought and filled a bathtub full with ice. They then took all my clothes off and dumped me into it to keep me alive. Incredibly, I survived! (God kept His word to never leave me nor forsake me.)

Now you'd think that would have cured me. But it didn't! Somehow, though, I thought I ought to go to church, and so I started going to this church in Costa Mesa called Calvary Chapel. But, before I went, I'd take LSD and then go hear this man, Chuck Smith, talk about Jesus coming back. I was so stoned that when I got home I'd think I was Jesus. Well, unknown to me, the Lord wasn't going to let that happen for very long. He had ways of convincing me this wasn't what I needed or wanted.

At eighteen I met this beautiful lady named Anna. She was looking for drugs, and since I had what she wanted, we soon became very close. But we never actually knew each other. For the next three years we were so stoned, we didn't know who we were. We had no life. We just existed from one day to the next. During that time I got busted twice and the second time was sentenced to jail for a whole year for selling drugs.

Prison caused me once again to hear the voice of the Lord from deep within my heart; I rededicated my life to Him, and having a captive audience, decided to preach to my inmate friends. But, without any real knowledge of who Christ was and no real foundation under me, and not knowing truly what I was talking about, I wasn't very effective. Also, there was no visible example that what I was talking about was a part of me. I never read the Bible, never prayed, etc. and because of that, the very day I got out (with the intent of sharing Christ with my friends and Anna) I really blew it. Instead of cruising with Christ, I crashed. You can't melt hearts for the Lord with your mind frozen in PCP. I should have been brain dead, but once again, the Lord got me out of the pit and spared my life.

About six months later Anna and I moved in together. Now you might ask yourself, "How can a born-again Christian be doing drugs, move in with a girl, etc.?" Well, as I'd said, I'd asked the Lord into my life, but that's all I had done. It was all lip service. Kind of like being adopted into a family and not learning their language; not living with them and getting to know them and what they're like or what their standards are.

Without Christian fellowship, the Bible, church, etc. I was "on ice," so to speak. They were the fuel I needed to ignite the fire of the Spirit within the frozen furnace of my heart. I had no power to grow, to overcome the things that held me in bondage, but God kept His promise. He never let go of me. One day I felt led to take Anna to Calvary Chapel and, while there, she got saved at a Love Song concert. We lived together for almost the next seven years, and during that time tried going to a church in Santa Rosa, but we always felt guilty and condemned. (Could it be because I was still drinking and smoking pot even though Anna had quit?) Nevertheless, people kept trying to conform us into their image. We finally got so frustrated with it all that within one day we ran and moved to Kings Beach, Lake Tahoe. We didn't tell any of our friends where we were because we didn't want to ever see them again.

With the condemnation and guilty feelings behind us, we sort of coasted along with each other for about three years when, in February of 1979, we heard about a church that met at a Kings Beach elementary school. We were told, "No stained glass windows, no organs, no hymns; just a guitar player with up-to-date music you'll enjoy and a very young pastor named Brian Larson who's funny and teaches the Word." Well, we decided to try it at least once and were quite surprised. We left that church just knowing that Jesus loved us! There was no guilt, no condemnation, just pure love. We agreed we would go back there again to see if it would be the same. The following week there was no doubt. We both knew that God loved us and that this was where He wanted us.

Now Anna and I were still not married, but we never told the pastor or anybody else. Little by little things began to change. We went to church every

Sunday, and I started reading the Bible and praying. We learned more and more about Jesus, the ice in my heart began to melt, and our love for Him and for each other deepened. As it did, I developed a desire to express that love, and picked up my guitar and began playing songs for the Lord. Then one day as I was reading a passage in First Corinthians, chapter seven, my eyes froze on a particular passage. In verse eight it said, "It is better to marry, than to burn." The words "burned" within me.

"Wow!" I said to myself, I certainly don't want to burn, and so I turned around and looked at Anna, and with emphasis said, "We need to get married."

To my surprise, she very calmly said, "Sure."

That was on Thursday, and our first mid-week Bible study was that night. I was totally convicted, and at the end of the study went to Pastor Brian and said, "I have a problem."

He said, "What's that?"

"Anna and I are not married."

To my surprise he didn't give me a sermon or a lecture. He just put his arm around me, and with a smile said, "We can take care of that."

I was elated and said, "Yeah, we can take care of that," and Pastor Brian married us on January 4, 1980, seven years to the day we'd moved in together.

Incredibly, the moment we said "I do," I was miraculously delivered from all drugs, smoking, and sexual immorality; everything I was trying to quit on my own strength for years. Anna and I felt as if twenty thousand pounds suddenly left our shoulders, and the next day God gave me a scripture which said, "To obey is better than sacrifice." which further confirmed the fact that out of my simple obedience to Him, He took care of everything I'd struggled with for so long.

We were excited and decided we wanted to do something to serve the Lord. We started two ministries, a rock band called Heartbeat, and a dance ministry called Sonrise Dance Team. Both of them flourished until 1986 when, because of sin in the band, Heartbeat broke up. Anna and I were devastated. We had invested six and one-half years in Heartbeat and thought, *What do we do now?* In earnest, we sought God with all our strength because we didn't know what to do. While waiting and praying, God spoke to my heart and said, *I want you back where you started in the music ministry with Calvary Chapel, leading worship.* That thought prompted my attendance at my first Calvary Chapel worship conference in Southern California where I was enlightened in many areas about what God wanted from us.

I remember Terry Clark's words that day that said something like, "God wants you to live with your heart in heaven, but to commute down here below, to do the work that needs to be done; then, at night, go back with Him in heaven."

What an impact that made in my life. I began seeking the Lord with my entire being, and my prayer was, "Lord, I want to know You, I want to worship You, I want to love You. And I don't know if I really do. Do I sing these songs and not mean them? I want to mean them." After the worship conference, I was inspired to start a Tuesday night meeting called Just for Worship at our home.

Six months later, I woke up one morning and I was stunned. I found that I couldn't move certain parts of my body. I was at least one-half paralyzed! Within three days I was a quadriplegic, completely paralyzed (or you could say "frozen") from the neck down. There had been no warning, no previous illness, etc. and I was at a loss for words. And I began to ask God why.

Then, in the deep silence of the night, God spoke to my heart, and He said, *I thought you wanted to know Me.*

And I answered, "Yes, Lord, but heal me."

Night after night I'd call out to Him, and He would say, *I thought you wanted to worship Me,* and I'd say, "Yes, Lord, but heal me."

He would say, *I thought you wanted to love Me.* "Yes, Lord, but please heal me."

I couldn't see it then but my heart was more set on my being healed than on what I told Him I wanted. In other words, I didn't really mean the words I said or sang because the minute something was wrong, my focus was entirely on myself.

After fourteen nights of this ongoing verbal struggle between me and the Lord, a brother came in with a guitar. It was Tuesday, our Just for Worship evening, and this brother decided to do it in my hospital room. As he strummed the guitar and I began to sing, "I love you Lord," my eyes began to water and my heart melted, and with my entire being, I did just that. I forgot for several minutes about my illness and I worshipped Him, and I loved Him and in my heart told Him, *Lord, I can be paralyzed the rest of my life. I may never play the guitar again, but Lord I do love you. Please use me right where I'm at.*

That's when the miracle began. I can't explain it but I was instantly transformed within mind, heart, soul and spirit. It no longer mattered that I was paralyzed. I was ready to serve the Lord in any and all circumstances. His overwhelming love transfixed me in a state of euphoria such as I'd never known before. I experienced a love so unfathomable, not time or matter could penetrate it, and with it came that "peace that passeth all understanding." Within two months, as I continued to bathe in that incomprehensible compassion, I felt the Lord begin to reverse the paralysis and I began to get better. But it was a slow process, almost two entire years. However, during those years, I really came to know the Lord as my God and Savior and the Lord of my Life. He was answering my prayers over and beyond anything I could have imagined. All our financial needs were met. When you see your bills continually being paid, even when you and your wife aren't working, you know you're in the middle of a miracle. "Seek first His kingdom and His righteousness, and all these things will be given to you as well" (Matt. 67:33). And were they ever!

Toward the end of those two years Jim was completely back to normal. He and Anna knew God had plans for them and by faith in 1988, they started a group called Truckee Graphite. A youth pastor by the name of Eddie Van Eyck came up with the name after asking them to do some special Christmas music for his youth group. And, since no other Christian group had that name, they decided to keep it. Right after that, Ron Hall, another pastor, asked them to play for their Sweetheart's Banquet. Thereafter, they received several invitations to perform at a singles retreat, a kids camp at Lake Tahoe, and Friday Night Singles, after which Jim prayed "Lord, if there is fruit in this ministry and You want this, Thy will be done."

And it absolutely was done because shortly thereafter, the Lord put Jim in the position of Music Minister at Calvary Chapel of Truckee, and in 1992 gave him the privilege of being one of the Assistant Pastors of that church. In addition, He blessed the dance ministry. The Sonrise Dance Team became the Sonrise Dance Company. Anna originally began with only adults because she'd been afraid to work with little ones. But the Lord kept tugging at her heartstrings to include the children. "Let the little children come to me, and do not hinder them, for the kingdom of heaven belongs to such as these" (Matt. 19:14). In obedience, Anna stepped out in faith and today has a ministry incorporating both adults and children, one of whom had the privilege of performing all over the United States and even Europe.

According to Anna, dance is a vehicle and means of expressing love to the Lord; an instruction of worship in which to express a little bit more of what's inside. It is a means of leading you into that place of knowing the Creator, and in your dancing, exhibit the fact that you want to serve Him and love Him with everything that is in you. Matthew 22:37 says, "Love the Lord your God with all your heart and with all your soul, and with all your mind."

Anna's goal for her students is to make sure their focus is first and foremost their love for God, and to worship Him for who He is; to acknowledge that dance is secondary, but definitely a vehicle that can bring others into the presence of God. In other words, she wants them to fully realize that they are not to worship the dance, but to use it to bring worship to God. Her emphasis is on the fact that it's not how good a dancer you are that counts, but rather someone who will touch the very heart of God so others will sense His presence in their midst. She'd rather have five students who love the Lord, than a room full of prima donnas on an "ego twirl."

As both Jim and Anna continued to put God first, He continued to bless, and their ministries, as well as those of the church, began to expand. After being invited to do a March for Jesus in Sacramento, doors opened for one in Reno, Nevada. Thereafter, the Lord graced them with the privilege of leading continuing marches. Their fire for the Lord was so prevalent they were called to minister in different denominational churches, in parks, at weddings, retreats, the Nevada State Fair, and even overseas. Their second trip to the Philippines took place in January 1999.

How about you? Where are you? Are you on fire for the Lord, or is He "on ice" in the frozen chambers of your heart? In Revelation 3:20 He said, "I stand at the door and knock, if anyone hears my voice and opens the door, I will come in." Will you open the door of your life and let Him in? It's your choice. If you don't, you can be sure the day will come when the frozen chambers of your heart will not only melt, but burn in a lake of fire for which there is no life preserver. Jesus said, "I am the way, the truth, and the life; no one comes to the Father except through me" (John 14:6). If you would like to turn your life over to the Lord just, by faith, believe Jesus' words, and pray the following prayer: Dear Jesus, I open the door of my heart to You. Please come in, forgive my sins, and take control of my life. I received You as my Savior and Lord, and ask You to fill me with Your Holy Spirit and accept me as your child.

Chapter Seventeen

SPECIAL CHILD

"I'm not a wretch! I'm special."
Janna Schlag didn't know how special, special was until she discovered the difference between profession and possession.

※

When the doctor discovered Mom had a severe kidney infection he recommended an abortion. It was her life or mine. Confused and frightened, Mom sought the prayers of Gumpo (my dad's dad) a man she considered a saint on earth. Gumpo convinced her to hold on. He believed by faith, that with God's help, we'd both make it. In the end God honored Gumpo's faith and the only thing that died was Mom's left kidney.

Dad, my two uncles and Grandpa Gumpo shared a medical practice in the small town of Faribault, Minnesota. I remember my small plastic doctor's bag. It was just like Dad's, only mine was filled with candy pills. Sometimes I'd dress up in a nurse's outfit with a cool hat that had a big red cross on it and a dark blue cape. I loved going on hospital visits and seeing the smiles on patients' faces as we walked into their rooms. Dad always held their hands, emphasizing the importance of touch as a part of healing, and handholding made you feel special. He taught me early on that it was important to love, serve, and respect everyone. He said this was the purpose of a good life.

Many of the people Dad took care of couldn't afford their medical treatment but Dad took care of them anyway. I felt so proud that my dad treated everyone regardless of cost. I recall one incident in particular that occurred years later when my best friend, Abby, told me how she cried when she got the bill for the lump my dad had removed from her breast; the amount was $0.00. Dad's selfless love made no small impact on his patients, and at Christmastime each year, they responded with handmade wall hangings, homemade candies, jellies, bins of nuts, etc., many times more than we knew what to do with.

Whether summer or winter, I was always happy. My best friends lived close by and there were always fun things to do. Sunday mornings found me sitting in a big chair with my sisters reading the comics to me. The fact that my family and friends made me feel so loved and so special made it easy for me to believe that there was a good God who loved me and that I was His special child. Every new person I met confirmed that feeling because they'd say, "Oh, you're Doctor Meyer's daughter. He was so good to me when I was sick. It's so nice to meet you."

Wow, I was the daughter of someone special! And yet, although no one ever said anything, I kind of noticed that I looked different from everyone else. There were dark circles around my eyes and I had very white skin with big freckles on my nose. My teeth seemed exceptionally big and bright yellow from the medication Mom had to take to save her life and mine before I was born. But, because of that special feeling, I didn't dwell on my appearance. I loved going to church and singing my heart out, dressed in that purple robe and white smock, the attire for the junior choir. One of my dearest memories was running to the bell tower at the end of service with my friends and ringing the giant bell that lifted us off our feet multiple times.

As I grew older, I read from the Scriptures and was given the privilege of lighting the candles as an acolyte. Whenever I read from the Bible to the congregation, I seemed to sense a special power, a bold ability from the Lord. What was that feeling? (I didn't know it then, but that feeling was the Lord; He was wanting those words to come from within my heart and not just from my lips.) You see, I was proud to read those words but only because my life was still very much centered on me. God was trying to tell me He was missing in my life.

When Andrew Lloyd Webber's *Jesus Christ Superstar* came out, I got lost in my headphones listening to the music just enthralled with the life of Jesus. Yet, when my brother and sisters used to sing "Amazing grace how sweet the sound that saved a wretch like me," I couldn't understand this song or the grace it proclaimed because I didn't feel like a wretch. Wretch? What's a wretch? Certainly not me; I'm not a wretch! I'm special. I just couldn't comprehend.

During junior high my sweet Grandpa Gumpo died and we moved to a much larger town so Dad could focus on his surgical expertise. Leaving my comfort zone (where I'd been known and loved for so long) wasn't easy, nor was it easy for me to approach the new girls at my school who stood around in a circle criticizing other classmates. However, it didn't take long for me to be in the popular group again, especially when the cutest boy in the class made it known that my dad had money and that we owned two Mercedes and an airplane. Until then I never knew that one type of car was more expensive than another.

In ninth grade things changed. All the different junior highs merged into the high school and it became a cruel competition to be popular, and I didn't feel so very special anymore. I found friendships to be painfully awkward until I began playing drums in the varsity band where I made some good friends. It was during this time that I met Lee "The Bee" Johnson. He was part of a group called the Modern Jazz Quartet. He asked me to play in his band and I had the time of my life with him. When he went off to join the Army Band, after graduating a year ahead of me, he wrote the most incredible and creative love letters. He talked a lot about God and his faith and would include Scriptures for me to look up. I'd never really read or understood the Bible, but I'd find quotes from various passages for him to look up when I wrote him back. I couldn't figure out why he said that was so important to him, but I was about to find out.

One very cold night in January, Lee drove all the way from Fort Carson, Colorado to Minnesota just to spend the weekend with me. That made me feel extra special. That night, he fervently and passionately shared his love of the Lord with me. He told me, "It isn't enough to just believe in God; you need to know Jesus and to ask Him into your heart and life." He told me of all the incredible things God had done in his life and how the Lord had used him in miraculous ways.

Wow! I thought. *I want that too.* That night I read my Bible intently for the first time and tried to understand it. The next morning I arose early and went to church with Lee. We attended services at my church first. There was no organ or choir, just a cappella singing from the congregation. For some reason I started to cry when we sang "Holy, holy, holy." Later that morning we drove over to Lee's nondenominational church. We sat in the front row. I noticed that there were people from all walks of life there. As the worship music began, I was enveloped by the power and presence of God, and in that moment, for the first time, I felt that God was real and that He knew each and every person.

Until now, I had always thought I was a good person but now all I could see and sense was God's goodness. When the service ended, I went to the back room where people prayed for me to receive the Holy Spirit. What an awesome experience that was. I can remember thinking and praying, *Jesus, you are for real; really really real! Thank you for showing me how much you love me. I want you; I need you. Please come into my heart and have your way with my whole life, and fill me with your Holy Spirit.*

I have never been the same again. I had an insatiable desire to read the Bible; it came alive to me. I couldn't stop reading, and it all suddenly made sense to me. I marveled at the grace of God and couldn't stop talking about His awesomeness. My parents thought I was involved in a cult or being fed misinformation. I also had an intense desire to be baptized publicly and almost immediately noticed one other thing that when I said a harsh word to my mom, or had a bad attitude, I felt inwardly ugly and awful! That special song began to make sense. It truly was His amazing grace that saved a wretch like me. To this day I love that song because it reminds me that His sacrifice at Calvary paid for my wretchedness, and I no longer have to worry about it because it was nailed to the Cross. I really was a wretch, but now I was His special child, and once again the daughter of someone special. I was special to my earthly father and now also to my heavenly Father.

Having the Lord in my heart and life, I believe, is what enabled me to pursue the goals and withstand the obstacles that lay before me. "Apart from Me, you can do nothing" (John 15:5).

My high school years were difficult; it was during that time that Mom and Dad were divorced after twenty-five years of marriage.

Once in college, I busied myself with trying to figure out what to do with my life. My parents never gave me much feedback on what I was good at, only that I could do anything I wanted. I loved music and photography but also thought perhaps I should be a doctor and crammed a four-year pre-med program into two and one-half years. At graduation, I was exhausted and tired of everything. I asked God if it was possible to use my biology and science degree and combine them somehow with my love of music and photography. Only God would know how to answer such a crazy prayer. "All things are possible with God" (Mark 10:27). He faithfully answered in a way I never expected. I was accepted as an assistant researcher on a sail and study program, analyzing the songs of humpback whales and photographing their tail flukes.

However, for the first time in my life I worked in a very isolated environment. I continued to pray, read my Bible, and listen to Christian music, but had no fellowship for months on that ship. But in my loneliness, God was with me. He instilled within me a desire for Christian leadership. He showed me the need for Christian leaders, and I prayed He would make me a leader for His own sake so others might be drawn to Him. That's exactly what He wants us to do, draw others to Him. Well, He answered that prayer also in a way I didn't expect. He said, "As the heavens are higher than the earth, so are my ways higher than yours" (Isa. 55:8), but I discovered they prepare us for His ultimate purpose to His glory and our joy.

This answer began with the position of leading a team of student researchers. First I led a small group, then a group of one hundred fifty or more on whale watch excursions. Those followed with a position giving slide shows and narrations to over two thousand passengers on cruise ships. Time after time I sensed the Lord giving me more courage and confidence. Knowing my previous self-centeredness, however, He kept me humble by letting the focus be on the whales, eagles, or glaciers, the real stars of the show. But He was building me up for a reason that He would reveal later.

By 1990 I'd been away from home a very long time and I dearly missed my family. I still wasn't sure of what to do with my life or where to settle down. Mom kept suggesting that I think about ministry. Well, I'd never thought about ministry as a career and dismissed her suggestion, thinking I was simply a Christian who loved God, not someone who would be called into a strange mission field. But her suggestion did bring to mind Father Crosby who years earlier had also suggested I think about ministry. It also brought to mind the fact that I lived in a house that was located right at the base of an evangelical, nondenominational seminary called Gorden-Conwell. *Hmmm,* my thoughts continued. *Perhaps I could meet a young man here who had the same heart for the Lord that I had.* (You see, deep down, I desired a special someone to share my life and the Lord's goals with me.) Well, I promptly enrolled in Christy Wilson's Evangelism of World Religions and Cults; the single most exciting class I'd ever taken. Each week we were assigned to witness to a different cult or church, and every week the most amazing testimonies came from our class experiences. Miracles happened; lives were given to Christ. As part of the class, we also had the honor of working for the Billy Graham Evangelistic Crusade, and in one night I had the awesome privilege of leading five people to Christ. Was the Lord answering my prayer to be a Christian leader that would draw other people to Him? Yes, and in ways of course again, that I never expected.

As a leader, however, my training had just begun. I had to be aware of the tricks of the enemy. In order to be a good leader, you have to go through boot camp. A general doesn't become a general unless he has first gone through the rugged ranks of training and experienced the unexpected attacks of the enemy. Like him, I had to learn how to overcome and conquer. While still at the seminary, the Lord showed me an absolute necessity. I was totally unaware of wolves in sheep's clothing, and so a very difficult lesson in discernment was on its way. I discovered that not everyone who says he is a Christian is one. I realized that professing Christ doesn't mean that you necessarily possess the Spirit of Christ. The Bible says that the enemy can appear as an angel of light.

Jim dazzled me with his knowledge of Scripture, what seemed remarkable insights, and most of all what I thought was his ability to lead people to the Lord. He would witness to people on the streets, at dinner, at gas stations, and even at stoplights. He was exciting to be around and would talk about the Lord until three in the morning. However, I soon discovered there was a very tormented and dark side to him. He truly was a wolf in sheep's clothing.

It began one evening when I told him I couldn't see him because of worship practice. As I was leaving practice, he showed up and spit in my face. He said it was because he loved me so much he always wanted to see me. From then it was all downhill. He always had an incredible explanation for his behavior that grew more and more abusive. To make a long story short, he abused me, tried to rape me, knifed my tires, etc. After a series of police reports and restraining orders, he vowed to kill both me and the dean of the seminary.

My pastor advised me to leave and move to another state to escape his grasp, and after graduating from seminary, that's what I did. I moved to Hawaii where I learned a few more lessons about discernment. My experience in trying to make these relationships work threw me into a deep depression. I had a hard time eating, and sometimes felt I couldn't even get out of bed, but then God in his amazing grace, as always, made a way. (God will make a way when there seems to be no way. He works in ways we cannot see. He will make a way for me.) I began playing worship music. The Lord was using my talent, the gift of music He gave me to minister to my weary heart, to remind me of His love and what a special daughter I was and still am, no matter what the circumstances. Day by day my joy and strength returned. Isaiah 43:19 says that God is able to make a roadway in the wilderness and streams in the desert.

Well, He made that roadway for me, a roadway into His very heart where streams of His love continue to flow to everyone that is thirsty and wants to come and drink As His special daughter, I got to claim His promise. "Delight yourself in the Lord and He will give you the desires of your heart" (Ps. 37:4), and He did. In addition to the joy of serving Him in my gifts of music and photography, He gave me that special man I'd been praying for. Steve had also been praying for his special partner right here on Maui; we met just north of Iceland on August 8, 1999.

Steve and Janna are married today. They share jointly in the ministry of drawing people to the Lord, not only in their church, but wherever they happen to be.

What about you? Janna thought she was a Christian until she realized the difference between profession and possession. Are you His special son or daughter? Are you a professor or a possessor? Remember telling everyone you're pregnant doesn't make you pregnant. Something has to happen! The visible eye doesn't see it happen but when it does, the results become obvious soon enough. Knowing Christ in your mind doesn't change your heart. God gives us a choice. You can know all about Him, and yet, not know Him. It's a matter of choice.

The Lord said, "I stand at the door (of your life) and knock. If anyone hears my voice and opens the door, I will come in" (Rev. 3:20). The only condition is that you have to be willing; willing to let Him love you, willing to accept His payment for your sins, willing to let Him give you a new beginning, a new life, and the assurance of knowing that you belong to Him forever and ever.

If that is the desire of your heart, I invite you to say the following prayer or a similar one of your choice, the Lord knows what's in your heart before you even begin: Dear Jesus, I open the door of my heart to you. Please come in, forgive my sins and take control of my life. I receive You as my Savior and Lord and ask you to fill me with Your Holy Spirit and accept me as Your child.

Chapter Eighteen

Status Symbol to Status Symbol

What is a crucible? Webster says it's a, "vessel of metal used for heating substances to high temperatures, a melting pot." That's where Bill DeCamp's life began in the crucible or melting pot of Bay Ridge, Brooklyn, near the New York City Waterfront (a far cry from Park Avenue).

※

In this overcrowded crucible of people, houses, kids and schools, I existed. During the depression there was an overabundance of everything except jobs, food, clothing, and things to do. Thirteen of us crowded into still another crucible—our house on 175th Street. It was here that Mom tried to do the impossible—feed eleven kids; seven boys and four girls. The absence of money wasn't as bad as the lack of food. It seemed we were always hungry. Dad's salary barely covered the meager portions Mom stretched from day to day. Like the story of the loaves and fishes in the Bible, she somehow accomplished the incredible. We knew nothing about God and there was no evidence of love in our house. Everyone in the area used foul language, and our home was no exception.

Mom and Dad had no time for the special attention we yearned for. In fact, they didn't have time for anything, not even discipline. We were out of control most of the time, and when my oldest brother took it upon himself to do the job by beating us, it was condoned by my parents because they felt somebody had to do it to keep us in line. I greatly resented the fact that Dad didn't discipline me himself. My anger and resentment festered and grew into a very aggressively bad attitude, most of which was directed at my dad. This caused many problems and yet, I believed that if my father had given me even one week of communication, it would have made a difference. I wanted recognition from him. All of us did. When your own father rejects you, it's hard to visualize acceptance from a heavenly Father.

In high school I majored in Harley Davidsons (definitely not on the curriculum) together with a few other things like stealing and street fighting, which was the norm for our neighborhood. At age fifteen I bought my first one-cylinder motorcycle. This became my status symbol. I rode it hard, fast,

Status Symbol to Status Symbol

and often. A cop blowing a whistle only meant open the throttle and lose the clown. I enjoyed my new position until the police stopped me—I never had a license. In spite of my status symbol however, I did manage to learn something, thanks to some very dedicated teachers. From PS 37 to Jamaica High I learned the academics and mechanics so desperately needed during this era. Mr. Eddy, our shop teacher, was a perfectionist who more than influenced me over the years. He discovered some undeveloped latent mechanical ability in me, and because of his persistence; four houses exist today in evidence of his teaching. Miss O'Brien, "the old war horse," took a personal interest in me. She was the one who went to the principal's office and got me back in school after I was expelled. She helped me find identification and purpose in school.

My first job brought new headaches. I used my paycheck to buy my own food, which Dad demanded I share with the other kids. I'd have done that anyway but because of his dictatorial and demanding attitude about what I was to do with my hard-earned money, I lost control and decked him. Mom asked me to go to the police department for counseling; the officer identified my problem as environmental, a result of my living conditions.

At seventeen I graduated and two years later I joined the Navy for adventure. I was on active duty for about five years. My bike was still my status symbol, my crutch. My attitude was the same and I was still a loner. Whenever someone talked to me about God or the Bible, I told them off in no uncertain terms. However, in spite of my bad attitude, continuous foul language, and motorcycle lifestyle, I managed to adhere to the routine, to regimen, and to discipline, and I was considered a good petty officer. In 1941 I was sent to the Philippines. It was there, looking at the business end of a Jap kamikaze, a split second before he exploded that I first realized how valuable life really was. Iwo Jima cracked my hard shell. When I saw men blown to pieces, it made me sick and I began to examine myself. I saw my total weakness and nothingness because they were dying en masse, and I wasn't. Just seeing this massive slaughter convinced me there must be somebody in charge. Having no other answers, I began reading the Bible.

When I left the Navy I bought a house in northern New Jersey. I continued to read the Bible even though I couldn't understand it because I was still searching. Meanwhile, I decided to settle down. I had known Helen since our high school days. We resumed our relationship and eventually got married. Helen was very religious but didn't know much about the Bible. She used to think that just going to church was the answer and pitied me because all I did was read the Bible. As I continued to read, I became very familiar with the historical and literary content of the scriptures. (So did the Eunuch in the chariot in Acts 3:30-31, but he didn't understand what he was reading until Philip explained it to him).

Accordingly, I developed a great deal of head knowledge, but no "heart" knowledge. I remember one night when Mom had a stroke and she asked me to tell her about God and dying. All I could do was tell her was about the history of the Red Sea, about Noah, and how this person begat that person, etc. I was very frustrated that I couldn't tell her more. However, one evening Billy Graham's New York City crusade was being televised. As Helen and I watched, everything fell into place. All the pieces fit together, and I realized who Jesus Christ really was. When Billy Graham said Jesus Christ was God come in the flesh and asked us to give our lives to Him, I knew I had to. I wanted to, but my pride kept saying, *How ridiculous to kneel in front of a TV set.* Finally, I swallowed my pride, forced myself down to my knees, and together with Helen, prayed to receive Christ. Then, as if to make sure, I immediately went to my bedroom and there again, alone on my knees, told Jesus I wanted Him to be Lord of my life.

From then on things began to change, and I saw some of God's promises come true. I was given the privilege of preaching on Second Street and serving on the Union Gospel Mission in Sacramento for six years during which I helped with the construction of the new mission on Bannon Street. I was tempted with many lucrative opportunities to go back to my former lifestyle but I no longer had any desire to do any of those things. "If anyone is in Christ, he is a new creation" (2 Cor. 5:17).

In 1969 while visiting my eighty-year-old dad in New York City, I asked his forgiveness and told him how, through the years, I'd regretted that evil act of striking him down. He listened to my testimony of Jesus, and I invited him to make Jesus Lord of his life. He did. He died two months later. (He could have died without Christ.)

I remember one particular incident while working at a gas plant in New Jersey. I was welding and became very thirsty. I had to pass between two sixty-foot tanks to reach the water cooler. Suddenly I stopped. An unseen force seemed to hold me back. Suddenly, the whole steel deck above me came crashing down in the place I would have been standing. "Never will I leave you; never will I forsake you" (Heb. 13:5).

As a result, I began witnessing more and more. I bought an Airstream trailer and traveled all over the United States. We finally settled in Auburn, California where I bought some acreage. That's where my new status symbol stands—a seventy-foot antenna tower at the sixty-foot level on Highway 49, where one can plainly see the John 3:16 spanning ten feet in length in evidence of what our wonderful Lord Jesus did with this beggar when He lifted him out of dunghill to set him among princes. I had retired as a pipe fitter/welder from Sacramento's Local 447 and now, during the day, I use this radio antenna to reach all over the world for Christ. When I make a contact, I send them information on how they can know Christ. At night, my status symbol, John 3:16

as bright as the beam from a lighthouse beckoning ships, calls out its message to highway travelers. It says, "For God so loved the world that He gave His one and only Son, that whoever believes in Him shall not perish but have eternal life."

Your status symbol reflects your lifestyle. What lifestyle does yours reflect? Will it bring you eternal life? If not, why not consider letting the Lord be your status symbol by inviting Christ into your heart and life. You can use your own words, or the following prayer: Dear Jesus, I open the door of my heart to You. Please come in, forgive my sins, and take control of my life. I receive You as my Savior and Lord and ask You to fill me with Your Holy Spirit and accept me as Your child.

Chapter Nineteen

Jodi's Rocky Soil

Jodi Kuhnmuench

That was the ultimate bottom! I knew I couldn't go on this way. My life had been one mess after another and it had to change if I was to survive!"

Police copters were flying overhead as I clutched the butcher knife in my hand. I had put one of our two dogs outside the house while I kept the other close by, but I was still afraid of what I couldn't see. I could only imagine who or what might be out there waiting for an opportunity to break in. This was only one of many terrifying nights for me.

There were five in our family, but it seemed I was always the one left home alone even though my brother was two years older. He had a learning disability that kept him from getting good grades, but he meant a lot to me and had an incredible talent; a genius who loved cars and knew just about everything there was to know about them. Our parents loved parties and we went to lots of them. Most of them were full of violence, and alcoholism was very prevalent. Mom sometimes drank too much, and Dad was a confirmed alcoholic who I rarely got to see.

When I was thirteen, Mom and Dad were divorced and our situation grew constantly worse. My younger sister began smoking and driving a car when she was just eight. I was the middle kid, extremely shy, and withdrawn. Also, being taller and skinnier than most kids my age, I was teased mercilessly. My room became a daily hideaway from painful fears and endless rejections. This continual pattern of isolation was not good but no one seemed to care. I continued to avoid family and friends and by eleventh grade stopped going to school altogether. I used to write excuses and sign my mother's name to them. No one seemed to notice that I was gone. I didn't drink, do drugs, or party so I'd wander aimlessly around the neighborhood or just sit around the house. At the end of eleventh grade I got caught. All the notes I'd forged sat in a huge pile on the principal's desk. School authorities suggested a psychologist, but I put up such a fuss they never forced me to go.

During twelfth grade I was told I'd never graduate. I couldn't face the embarrassment and just wanted to get out of Los Angeles. To my surprise, Mom agreed to move because all the kids were running wild. My grandparents, who lived in Grass Valley, California, invited us to stay with them. Was I ever thrilled when I discovered graduation requirements were lower there. A guy in my new school invited me to go to something called Young Life, and during the summer of my senior year, I accepted Christ at one of their meetings, but no one took the time to help me to know who He really was or to really understand what this decision meant.

The Bible says in Matthew 13:19 (NASB), "When anyone hears the word of the kingdom and does not understand it, the evil one comes and snatches away what has been sown in his heart so that he may not believe and be saved. This is the one on whom the seed was sown beside the road."

Graduation day finally arrived. I was excited. It seemed an angel sat on my shoulder as I received my diploma. This was the happiest day of my life. After that, all I wanted to do was ski, and I got that opportunity when, on Christmas Eve, I was offered a job at the Sugar Bowl in Tahoe, California. I was only seventeen, but Mom drove me up there on Christmas Day to start work.

When the season ended, I went back to Grass Valley. A friend invited me to go on a double date with her but I didn't want to because I grew up with the idea that sex was what people did to you if they liked you, and so had early on accepted sexual promiscuity as the normal thing to do. I didn't know any different. My friend was always very popular and always had boyfriends. She wanted me to be just as popular and so kept insisting that I go. I finally gave in and that night I got raped. Fear, pain, and confusion left me temporarily paralyzed. I was in shock and unable to think. I didn't know what to do, so I did nothing. Well, the next morning Mom found out where I was. She didn't know what had happened but she dragged me out of the house and took me home. She didn't speak to me for about a week and then said, "If you're going to do that (spend the night at some guy's house) you might as well live with him, and you're out of here." So I was kicked out and I went to live with this guy in a rat-infested trailer. He was a drug dealer and a very explosive individual. So I didn't argue when he wanted me to go on drug runs with him.

We weren't together very long when I got word that my brother was killed in a car accident. At his funeral, my mother began to pray. She had never done that before. When she got on the plane to come home she told my step dad that she wanted to go to church. I don't know what happened at church but from that moment on she stopped drinking and smoking; she had a very dramatic conversion.

My brother's death left me emotionally crashed. I lost all control and had incredible anxiety attacks. Sometimes I'd go running through the streets at night completely out of my head. My boyfriend would tackle me and hold me down so I wouldn't go wandering off and wake up in a park or something. I tried seeing a county psychologist but on my way to his office I almost lost my voice, and his suggestion to participate in group therapy was so terrifying I never went back. When my boyfriend was sent to jail on a hit and run charge, I decided to drive back to Grass Valley. I thought that would end his threats and the bizarre relationship we had. But he continued to harass me until I met Jim, my first husband.

Jim and I moved back to Tahoe and lived together for almost a year. He was an alcoholic too and very violent. If something didn't go his way he'd fly into a rage and once almost killed himself. When we moved to San Diego; his family insisted we get married. I didn't want to; he said my fears were just pre-wedding jitters. He smoked pot and drank while I went to work. We kept moving and I kept thinking that *If I move, things will get better*, but they never did. I kept trying to fill the emptiness in my life and found myself wandering around in an emotional daze once again. We finally decided to move back to Grass Valley so I could be near Mom.

She surmised something was wrong when she never saw any food in our refrigerator but plenty of beer. My parents tried to talk to Jim about that one night but he flew into a rage and threw them out.

Mom began taking me to Alanon as well as to church. Once again, I went forward and even got baptized, thinking that baptism would make a difference, but it didn't. "And the one on whom seed was sown on the rocky places, this is the man who hears the word and immediately receives it with joy; yet he has no firm root in himself, but is only temporary; and when affliction or persecution arises...immediately he falls away" (Matt. 13:20, 21 NASB).

I tried reading the Bible in my room while Jim drank in the living room. He was in complete denial of his problem and wouldn't talk to me. When I suggested separating for a while to give us time to think, he wouldn't even discuss it. Once again, smoldering emotions were about to erupt. Mom saw that I was out of control, and she was afraid of what I might do. She sensed my suicidal tendencies and for the first time, realized I'd contemplated suicide on several other occasions. So, she came over and said, "You're leaving; you need to get out of here." They told me to pack my bags, but when they saw that I couldn't even cope with that simple task, they packed my things and took me home with them. Two weeks later I discovered I was pregnant.

Mom had me stay with her until after the baby was born. Jim came by occasionally but his attitude never changed. I began spending a lot more time reading the Bible; it brought peace to my mind and heart. I also discovered that Jim's emotional games and threats didn't affect me anymore. I felt safe and believed God was watching out for me. After Trevor was born I thought things would be different but they weren't. Jim left and I never saw him again. I eventually filed for divorce, and the Lord gave me a good job using my artwork. For some reason I still felt the need to go to church, and I volunteered to teach the two-year-olds in Sunday school. I had lots to do, but I was lonely. I was the only single mom in the church, yet no one seemed to understand my need for friends, nor did they seem to care.

My heart ached for companionship. When I didn't receive it, I feasted on anger, self-pity, and sarcasm. I kept thinking *Oh, I'm good enough to teach and baby-sit, but not good enough to be invited to special events and other fellowships.* I felt sorry for myself and decided to do something just for me, and I did. I went dancing almost every night and little by little, my new friends encouraged me in things I should not have been doing. My rebellious pity party lasted about nine devastating months. The only good thing that happened during that time was meeting Andy. We were introduced to each other at my friend's wedding. Andy seemed really interested in me, and guests and the reception faded into the distance as we talked. Unknown to us, the weather changed several times as well. It rained, snowed, and even hailed during our conversation, but we never noticed. It was evident to all that we were oblivious to everyone and everything around us from the moment we met, and we took no small amount of teasing for it.

Andy made me feel special. I had a wonderful time and what a wonderful reprieve from the frustrations in my life. But the day ended, Andy was gone, and reality returned. With it came the anger and bitterness and an urge to get even. I wanted to do everything to men they had ever done to me. I'd been the victim and was now bent on lashing out at them. All I wanted to do was hurt others. All it produced was more hurt, more pain. Nothing was accomplished by it, nor did it give me what I was searching for.

I had no peace for weeks and was very restless. I became greatly troubled by what I was doing and then suddenly, I remembered Andy and how nice he had been to me. I decided to go back to Truckee, California to visit the friend who got married. She got in touch with Andy and arranged a meeting at the Truckee rodeo. We started dating, but once again, I got into a promiscuous relationship. When a girl from work invited me to a Bible study, I was convicted about the way Andy and I were living, but I was already worried and in trouble. "And the seed which fell among the thorns, these are the ones who have heard and as they go on their way, they are choked with worries...and bring no fruit to maturity" (Luke 8:14 NASB).

I'd discovered I was pregnant again and went through an incredible mental and spiritual battle.

Jodi's Rocky Soil

Being too week and emotionally drained to deal with the pregnancy, I found myself in an abortion office. That was the ultimate bottom! I knew I couldn't go on this way. My life had been one mess after another and it had to change if I was to survive.

As Andy and I continued to see each other and began falling in love, I decided that I truly wanted a new life. This meant an earnest commitment on my part, and I started taking steps in that direction. I told Andy I was going to go to church and wouldn't sleep with him anymore. Also, that I wasn't going to party or drink anymore; I was going to give it all up and sincerely and wholeheartedly committed my life to the Lord completely. "And the seed in the good soil, these are the ones who have heard the word in an honest and good heart, and hold it fast, and bear fruit with perseverance" (Luke 8:15 NASB).

I thought he would say, "See you later. Nice knowing you." Instead he started going to church and reading the Bible with me. After a little while Andy received and accepted Christ and made a commitment to also walk with the Lord. His commitment, unlike my first two, was sincere and rooted in good soil right from the beginning. He proposed to me almost immediately after that, and I accepted. We couldn't afford a wedding so we eloped and took my son, Trevor with us. We drove to the South Shore, got married, and then moved to Tahoe where we began going to Calvary Chapel of Truckee.

Our first few years together were rough because the past continued to haunt me, but the Lord knew that when he brought Andy into my life. Andy came from a very large, stable midwestern family with no history of divorce. God knew he was just the balance I needed to conquer the rocky soil in my life. Through Andy I learned to trust and obey God and walk by faith. The last few years have been an incredible time of healing for me. Every now and then, depending on the situation, I used to still flip out, expecting to wind up separated or divorced. But Andy would put an arm around me and say, "Hey nobody is going anywhere. We're together and we are one with the Lord."

And so we made it a habit that whenever things started going wrong, Andy and I would get on our knees and pray; that's when miracles happened. When a husband and wife are on their knees before the Lord, they are tied with Christ in a three-fold cord. "A cord of three strands is not quickly broken" (Eccl. 4:12).

God has blessed us incredibly and in His mercy gave us another son, Jordan. We've been married twelve years now and have two healthy happy sons. Because of God's unfailing love during the many years I shut Him out of my life time and time again, I learned the meaning of parental love and patience. He never gave up on me. It's awesome to see the changes He's made in my life.

I know that I will still encounter situations that may cause me to slip but each day realize more and more that we are His and nothing can take us out of

His hands, and that He is faithful to finish the good work He began in us.

What about you? Is the soil of your heart ready to receive Christ? Are you willing to let the Holy Spirit remove the rocks and prepare it for Him" If you get serious with God, He will get serious with you. "Come near to God and He will come near to you" (James 4:8). "I am the way, the truth and the life. No one comes to the Father except through Me" (John 14:6). "Let us draw near with a sincere heart" (Heb. 10:23).

If you sincerely want the rocks removed and a new garden planted in your life just, by faith, pray the following prayer: Dear Jesus, I open the door of my heart to You. I invite you to come in, forgive my sins, and take control of my life. I receive You as my Savior and Lord and ask you to fill me with Your Holy Spirit and accept me as your child.

Chapter Twenty

I Just Want Them to Know Him!

Aaron Jones was only seven years of age when his heart ached to know the Lord. The Lord answered that ache through Aaron's curiosity and His Word.

※

My mom had an exceptionally busy work schedule, and when her friend Kaitee said she'd like to spend the afternoon with me, I was eager to go because the plan was to stop at MacDonald's for lunch. We were on our way from Truckee to Squaw Valley, about a fifteen-minute drive. We talked about different things including God and heaven. I was curious about that and so Kaitee began sharing things from the Bible with me. She happened to have a Bible in the car and we stopped and spent a bit of time reading in the first chapter of Genesis just before going into MacDonald's.

After that we went over to Kings Beach where we stopped at Paulie and Richard's store (they were friends of Mom and Dad). When we left there, Kaitee asked if I'd like to have a Bible to continue reading, and I said yes. So we went over to the Bible bookstore and she bought a Bible for me. She also bought a WWJD (What Would Jesus Do?) bracelet that I really liked.

When we got back into the car, she asked me if I wanted to ask Jesus into my heart and I remember I had a happy feeling and I thought, *Yes,* this was what I wanted to do, and I prayed, "Dear Jesus, I love You and I know that You love me. I know I'm a sinner and I'm sorry for my sins. Please come into my life, forgive my sins, and be my personal Savior. I give my life to You. Make me the kind of person You want me to be." After praying that prayer to invite Jesus into my heart and accepting him as my personal Savior, I still had a very happy feeling inside, and I could hardly wait until my mom and dad had that same feeling.

When we got back to Truckee and were back in the office, I told her, and she was happy, really happy.

As days went by and I started getting used to the fact that I had been saved, I noticed some very definite changes and differences in my attitude and thinking. I was no longer doing, nor did I feel like

I Just Want Them to Know Him!

doing, all the bad things I used to do, like breaking the rules in school. Another thing that changed was that I always used to argue with my parents and would be sent to my room and be grounded for my bad attitude. After I received Jesus, I would agree with them and if I didn't, it wasn't like before. I wasn't rebellious anymore.

I came to realize very strongly that if I sinned, it would be forgiven. (Before that, if I sinned, I felt I had to confess it to my parents and to God.) But now, after receiving Christ into my heart, I knew that I only had to confess it to the Lord because He knew it all anyway, and He had paid the price for it.

I had a great desire to go to church and when we moved to Auburn, I met a boy whose family went to this Christian fellowship church. Not long after that, my mom met his mom and we started going to that fellowship. They had children's church and it was more of like a Bible study church.

Other things I noticed was that when walking home from school sometimes, I'd see kids smoking, and I would ask my mother to help me pray for them. As days and weeks passed, I asked Mom once or twice if she knew the Lord. Then during about the second year we had been living in Auburn while she was driving the car, she turned to me and told me that she was saved. Then she called her parents to tell them about it too.

I've been trying to share Jesus Christ with my friend Kelly, and my dad. I just want them to know Him. Those are my goals for right now.

How about You? Does your heart ache to know the Lord? Would you like to notice some definite changes and thinking in your attitude? The Bible tells us that "If anyone is in Christ, he is a new creation; the old has gone, the new has come" (2 Cor. 5:17). If you want to invite Christ into your heart and experience this new life, you can pray the prayer Aaron prayed or you can use the following: Dear Jesus, I open the door of my heart to You. Please come in, forgive my sins, and take control of my life. I receive You as my Savior and Lord and ask You to fill me with your Holy Spirit and accept me as Your child.

Chapter Twenty One

Giant Hands

I was standing on the ground on top of some wet fill dirt with the control box between my hands when I accidentally ran the boom into a 7200-volt feeder line. Like a whip, electricity cracked through my body, jamming the box against my chest."

Rick Defer was dead for thirty minutes, but he didn't know it.

※

My dad graduated from San Quentin in 1958, the same year I graduated from high school. I never knew him but learned about him through my mom and step dad who tried to do the very best they could for me. It wasn't until I got older that I discovered he was a criminal. I got a taste of what that word meant when I was fifteen because even though I was a good student and athlete, I got into trouble and spent some time in a juvenile prison in Martinez, California.

After high school I moved to Los Angeles, California where I continued my education and met my first wife. By age twenty-one, I was a father and a fireman. We had marital problems and after two years were divorced. A few years later I married again but that also ended in divorce. I was granted full custody of the one and only child of this marriage, a son. Being a single parent wasn't easy but I was determined to do a good job.

During the course of the next few years some Christian friends kept hounding me until I finally accepted an invitation to listen to a scientist at the Brookside Golf Course in Pasadena, California. (A golf course seemed less intimidating than a church.)

This particular speaker shared his personal testimony about Christ from a scientific point of view. His words made no small impact on me and I was deeply touched by what he had to say. (God's Word is often referred to as the "sword of the Spirit.") Well, that night, you might say my heart was "pierced" by that sword. With tears in my eyes and everyone watching, I got up and walked outside. I looked up at the stars where I thought heaven was, and though I didn't know exactly what to say, I prayed, "Father, I want Your Son, Jesus, to come into my heart and be the manager of my life. I don't want to walk alone anymore." And then I apologized because I didn't know if that was the correct thing to say, and I ended it with an, "Amen."

As I wiped the tears away an incomprehensible peace came over me, which I understood as a, "Yes. It's OK, what you said."

To my surprise, however, my acceptance did not change me overnight. I still went to football games on Sunday instead of going to church. I still had a rather foul mouth and continued to drink and carouse just as I had before. But things did begin to change pretty rapidly after that.

When the fire department retired me because of several medical disabilities, I decided to move out of Los Angeles. Since I enjoyed the mountains, I decided to check out the Tahoe area. As I drove, I just kind of followed the highway and before long, I found myself in the town of Truckee. There was something unique about that old town that I couldn't resist. So, after buying a house in Tahoe Donner, I went back to get my son and we moved into our wonderful new home in 1978.

However, things didn't stay wonderful. In the spring of 1980 I took a job with North Tahoe Transit Mix. It was a good job and I was doing quite well until October 8, when I drove a fifty-foot boom to a jobsite at the top of Tahoe Donner on Alder Creek Road. After pumping concrete into the housing foundation, I accidentally ran the boom into a 7200-volt feeder line that feeds electricity to upper Tahoe Donner. I had been standing on the ground on top of some wet fill dirt with the control box between my hands. When the boom hit the feeder line, thousands of volts bolted into the control box. Like a whip, electricity cracked through my body. It contracted my biceps and jammed the box against my chest. The impact threw me to the ground where, according to witnesses, for five full minutes I thrashed around like an open-butted fire hose as electricity snaked through my body. People at the job site tried desperately to get the box off my chest but couldn't. When the line finally burned through releasing my body from its power, some people ran to check me out. There was no pulse; no breathing or movement of any kind.

I found out later that electricity entered my body at the sternum, traveled through and out of my right groin and upper thigh and also exited from the inside of my right knee and both feet. I had been wearing steel-shanked and steel-toed boots, which spread the electricity completely around my feet burning them severely.

After checking for respiration and finding none, they decided I'd been electrocuted the moment the electricity hit me. So they attempted no CPR, no mouth-to-mouth resuscitation, and left me for dead. Someone ran to a neighboring house to call for help. Some minutes later, paramedics arrived from Tahoe Forest Hospital. After listening to witnesses and checking me out, they too, decided that after all this time, (about thirty minutes) I was long gone. There was no CPR, no resuscitation, no defibrillation, and I was officially pronounced dead; I was, but I didn't know it. Incredibly, as I lay there, I was enjoying a feeling of love, peace, and serenity I'd never experienced before. Though I saw no bright lights or anything like that, I envisioned or had a sense of giant hands holding me very still. I was overwhelmed with the feeling that I was being cradled just like a baby in a mother's womb. I was contented, comfortable, and filled with joy as I floated in these giant hands. I experienced no pain, no panic, and had an unfathomable knowing that every thing was OK. Though I didn't think of heaven or anything like that, I had this inner recognition that was so strong, I just knew I was in the arms of the Lord. As I basked and reveled in those giant hands everything suddenly went blank and though I have no personal recollection of coming back to life, the paramedics and others gave me a recount of what they saw.

They said I suddenly sat up, threw off the sheet that had been placed over me, and started talking to the paramedics. (After thirty minutes without oxygen, this was unheard of.) My sudden resurrection caused no small reaction among those still at the scene. Though totally stunned and in awe, they began giving me first aid. After finishing their immediate treatment, I was transported to Tahoe Forest Hospital. According to witnesses there, I looked and acted very normal except for my burns. They said I was talking coherently and even cracking some jokes. From there, fixed wing aircraft transported me to Sacramento's UCD Medical Center.

When I woke up the next morning, I still couldn't recall anything except being cradled in those secure and wonderful giant hands and arms. But, from then on I remembered everything that happened to me and could've almost wished I were back in those arms. When I saw all the bandages, the IVs monitoring the pulse in my feet, and the electrical devices at my chest to monitor my blood pressure and pulse, I was overcome with emotion. The physicians were astounded by the fact that my pulse was normal. My blood pressure was perfect, 120/80, and even my internal functions were perfect. They could find no medical explanation for that. For me there was only one explanation, that when God protects you, He protects you.

The next day three young pastors, Eric, Tom, and Rob from Church on the Lake in Incline Village came to visit me. The doctors had given me large doses of drugs to ease the pain but they didn't work. After visiting awhile, we joined hands in prayer. Eric and Tom were holding my bandaged hands and Rob put his head on my right shin with both hands on either side of his head. As I closed my eyes I thought how weird it was for Rob to put his head on my leg. Eric was the first to pray, and within seconds I had the most astounding experience. I felt a very warm tingly sensation start at my feet and work up each leg, up through my torso, into my arms and my head, and out my hands. And, once again, I knew the Lord – by His Holy Spirit – was enveloping me because that same feeling of peace, serenity, and knowledge came upon me just as I had experienced when He cradled me. The pains in my chest, groin, feet, and hands disappeared. It was awesome! I was so astonished I opened my eyes in disbelief! When Eric finished praying, they each looked at their hands. They were red with the heat that had come through my body. Even Rob's forehead was red. We were all astonished because Eric and Tom were holding bandaged hands. They hadn't even touched my skin while they were praying. Rob, whose head was on my right shin, was the only one touching my skin.

Later that day the orthopedic surgeon and a herd of interns came into my room. UCD is a teaching university and my doctor was talking quite a bit about my unusual case. ("Unusual" is easier to say than "miraculous.") He shared with them how astonished they were that I was even alive. After that they determined they were going to amputate both my legs about seven to seven and one-half inches below my knees. I tried negotiating with them on that idea because it was just my feet that were burned. I saw no reason to cut off so much of good leg. To my dismay, I was quickly informed that it was the best length for the best fit for my future prosthetics if I were to walk again. But, he also said that because I had numerous exit areas on my right leg that they would examine the option of saving it, together with some of my right foot. That decision would be made during the surgery. Since he didn't seem very optimistic, I fully expected to have both my legs amputated. To my surprise however, only my left leg was amputated, seven and a half inches below the knee, and my right foot was only half amputated. For the next 16 days I traveled in and out of the burn unit for treatment.

However, there was no treatment to erase the after-shocks (words like "freak" and "cripple") that haunted me wherever I went. I had deep emotional feelings about where my life was going. What kind of life would I have? What was I going to be able to do? Would I ever ski again? I was missing part of a leg and a foot and very disfigured in several areas. Would a woman ever love me again? Could she look at me and not notice the ugly scars on my chest, and hands? I became so focused on my deformities that I became more of an emotional cripple than a physical one.

A few months later I developed an addiction to my pain medication. Without realizing it, I'd been doubling and tripling the dosage. When we take drugs, we need to recognize that medications, regardless of legality, are often addictive, and you can find yourself not thinking clearly anymore, resulting in a transition from the doctor's prescriptions to illegal drugs.

Marijuana was my first. I was quite apprehensive and fearful of cocaine but had no fear of marijuana because I'd experimented with it before. It helped with some of the pain and nausea that was initially corrected by the prescribed drugs. But I began feeling guilty and during my next visit to the doctor, shared with him that I was smoking dope. He said if it helped with my pain and nausea and I didn't have any other side effects, to go ahead and do it. So, I rationalized that it was OK. After all, my doctor said so, and I was a cripple and in a lot of pain. The problem was that the insurance company certainly wouldn't pay for marijuana, so I had to buy it. Little by little I found myself not caring, slipping more and more into illegal behavior and further into the criminal world. The young man who first talked me into drugs now offered to sell half of my stash to pay for it as my medication. So now all of a sudden, I became a dealer.

Smoking marijuana can cause you to like the feeling it gives you which adds to the irrational behavior of continuing to smoke it. Not too much later, my son-in-law offered me some cocaine and I took it without even batting an eye. This quickly pushed me into a much deeper involvement in the criminal community. Satan had really found a way to trap me and penetrate my Christianity. I had become what I termed a "Christian doper." (As I said before, Jesus saves us, but He doesn't take away our free will). Somehow, I couldn't stop loving the Lord and I continued to pray, but He was far from me. The drugs had severely short-circuited my prayer life. There were no answers, no blessings while I was doing drugs and eventually, I lost my home and my car. I had no job, no support from friends, family, or church.

After going through many different kinds of hospitalizations and withdrawals, I came to what I call the final event. I was taking a drug prescribed by a psychiatrist known as emempromine. This was supposed to help me quit my cocaine habit, but I became addicted to that too. One wintry day I ran out of emempromine and thought I was coming down with the flu, but it didn't take long to change my view from the flu to withdrawals. I called the doctor and explained the circumstances. He agreed that I was one of the unfortunate ones to have that kind of side effect from emempromine, but if I could get down to the hospital he'd give me a prescription for another drug to counteract his previous prescription.

Two things became abundantly clear. First, I was not capable of getting to the hospital. There was a raging blizzard outside and all I had was a bicycle. And second, I was trapped like a hamster in a wheel inside of a cage. So I told the doctor, "No thank you," and that I wouldn't be calling him anymore,

Giant Hands

and I prepared myself. I'd gone through withdrawals before and I knew what to expect. I stripped down to my shorts, brought in some firewood, placed a bucket on the coffee table, turned on the TV, and was ready to face it for however long it took. At the end of four days and nights of intense vomiting, pain, anger, depression, and all of the emotions that one could imagine, I suddenly remembered the book of Luke, and the story of the Prodigal Son. I had my doubts as to whether or not the Lord would take me back, but I had nowhere else to go and I was so purged and so exhausted after dozens of hours of vomiting into that bucket, that I lay back on the couch and said the following prayer: "Father, I'm so tired, I don't have the energy to give you one of those thee and thou preacher prayers. I just want to come back to you and I need some help. Amen."

To my astonishment when I woke up eighteen hours later, the blizzard was over, the sky was blue and dotted with puffy white clouds, and I had not frozen to death. As I shook the cobwebs out of my head, I remembered my prayer and realized that God had answered it. He knew my heart and knew I'd been sincere. I had an overwhelming feeling that I needed to do something to show an act of faith and an act of repentance for His mercy. At first I didn't know what, but I had to do something so I began gathering things around the house that were drug related – cocaine vials, minors, razors, haggles (I found some that still had drugs in them), and pipes for smoking marijuana. Amazingly, instead of smoking or snorting the drugs, I found my desire for them had disappeared. I held all of them in my hands and opened the door of the stove, which had a new fire in it and said, "Lord, this is my physical act of repentance and my thanks for hearing me." And I threw all of the drug paraphernalia into the fire. That was the first day of rest of my life.

Approximately two weeks later, I began to see those giant hands move in my behalf in a new and awesome way. However, though I now had a new future, I still had my drug-related past clinging to me like the placenta after a baby is born.

During my drug-related escapades, there had been several arrests, and I still had to face the consequences for those. Well, I enrolled in a vocational rehabilitation school, started working again, and in my spare time (believing the Lord would protect me) did some undercover work for four police agencies. After two years, I was finally called to trial for my previous arrests. The four police agencies, Washoe County Narcotics Unit, Nevada County Sheriff's Office, Placer County Sheriff's Office, and the DEA testified that they had never seen anyone more dedicated and more fruitful in helping them. The detective from Washoe County Narcotics testified that over eighteen criminals and many drug venders were prosecuted as a direct result of my activities, and according to the police, I was also the key factor in a murder case that would never have been solved had I not stood up as a witness.

Through all of this the Lord was loyal to me. I was never harmed even in the smallest way, and the nine serious counts pending against me were all dropped. I was allowed to plead guilty to one count of possession of marijuana and given probation of up to five years. I served two of those and then was miraculously kicked out of the system as completed. Some time later, in checking my records, I found that they had been expunged (as if they had never happened). The same thing happens when you give your heart to Christ, the past is "erased" as if it never happened, "If anyone is in Christ, he is a new creation. The old has gone, the new has come" (2 Cor. 5:17).

And for Rick, all things have truly become new. God is managing his life and he is not walking alone anymore. Incredibly, in spite of his handicaps, the Lord has given him a work to do that has led him all over North America. Those giant hands have opened doors of opportunity as a lay minister to many different people, especially firefighters for whom Rick has a great deal of respect. But they're only part of the outreach God has given Rick. He's had opportunities to share with people on airplanes as he travels from one state to another. On occasion he's invited to hospitals where he is able to encourage and share with other amputees, to show them how God loves them, and that there is a purpose for their lives. Sometimes he goes to other churches or groups to share the importance of placing yourself in the awesome and unfathomable hands of the Lord. Recently he had the joy and privilege of being the keynote speaker at a men's meeting in a Presbyterian church. He especially enjoys sharing in men's groups because he says it challenges them to be warriors for Christ.

What about you? Have you placed yourself in those awesome, gentle, giant hands of the Lord? If you were to die today, would you see Him picking you up and cradling you, carrying you with Him to Paradise, or would you see another set of hands pulling you into the arms of something too ugly and fiendish to describe; arms that drag you off to an intense chasm of fire and eternal darkness with no chance of ever seeing anyone or anything again – just eternal darkness and pain. The choice is yours; the giant arms of the Lord and eternal happiness, beauty, and light or the clawing, painful arms of death, darkness, and hell. Jesus said, "I stand at the door and knock, if anyone hears my voice and opens the door, I will come in." (Rev. 3:20). Jesus is referring to the door of your life. It is solely your decision; no one came make it for you.

If you want to place yourself in those giant hands of the Lord, and commit your life to Him, you can open the door and invite Him in by just praying the following prayer: Dear Jesus, I open the door of my heart to You. Please come in, forgive my sins, and take control of my life. I receive You as my Savior and Lord and ask you to fill me with Your Holy Spirit and accept me as your child.

To order additional copies of

Eternal Makeovers

Have your credit card ready and call:

1-877-421-READ (7323)

or please visit our web site at
www.pleasantword.com

Also available at:
www.amazon.com
and
www.barnesandnoble.com

Printed in the United States
93740LV00001B/58-75/A